Never Fear Conflict Again

Again

How to leverage conflict into intimacy

Ken Williams, PhD

Gaylyn R. Williams

Relationship Resources, Inc.

Colorado Springs, Colorado

Never Fear Conflict Again

Other versions of this book have been published in the following languages: Mandarin, Armenian, Spanish, French, Indonesian, Tamil (India), Hindi (India), Turkish, Arabic, Russian, Farsi (Iran), Korean, Russian, Hausa (Nigeria), German, Greek, Japanese, Portuguese, Tagalag (Philippines) and Vietnamese.

For information about Relationship Resources, Inc. or for quantity discounts:

    PO Box 62454, Colorado Springs, CO 80962
    Web: www.RelationshipResources.org
    Email: info@RelationshipResources.org

ISBN for the print book: 9781796468861

Library of Congress Control Number: 2019938783

Cover designed by: Debbie Lewis

Printed in the United States of America.

What People Are Saying
About this Material

This includes earlier versions of this material. Many names are removed to protect the people.

"Scripture is clear that the Lord cares deeply about how we treat one another, both within and outside the walls of the church. But too often relationships in some areas of our lives can feel difficult to navigate! In *Boost Your Relationship IQ* Gaylyn Williams wisely shares practical tools to build community by learning the skills to treat each other with dignity and love that is truly felt and understood. These biblically-grounded principles are destined to transform lives and ministries, unlocking new doors to spread the love of Jesus."

Dr. Dick Eastman, International President, Every Home for Christ

"We train people to preach so well that they can raise the dead, then they kill them again with their interpersonal skills. These materials give pastors and ministry leaders the practical skills they need to be effective in their ministries."

Patrick Repp, Minnesota Renewal Center

"I really believe this material has His anointing and is the best training tool I've seen for our kind of people. I really believe in it."

Duane, missionary in Thailand

"Talk is golden and now Gaylyn has unlocked the communication vault. You will never be able to walk the walk if you can't talk the talk! This course will give you the tools to become a gold-medal-winning people person."

Mark Walters, author

"I have three things to say about your material: 1) excellent 2) Excellent 3) EXCELLENT! It is definitely worth the price of the course!"

Phil, missionary in Ecuador

You've given us something that really can affect the kingdom of God."

A ministry leader

"I am really impressed with the training materials, depth and well-thought-out information."

Susan, Denver Seminary student

""Thank you for the clear, practical, biblical teachings. It is so freeing to be able to enter into a difficult and fragile situation."

A missionary in a creative access country

"Using the principles I learned about loving listening, I led someone to Christ!"

A missionary in Western Europe

About Workshops Using These Materials

Workshops using an earlier version of this book have been taught worldwide to over forty-thousand people.

"This is the most helpful, practical, meaningful and applicable workshop I have *ever* attended."

George Warren, Evangelical Free Church Mission

"I was so captured by this material that our Church was fortunate enough to host a week-long workshop. We all found it extremely helpful in equipping us in our ministry to others and it has been passed along to many others. Years later I still find the material beneficial in my personal ministry and as I equip others to minister. It is as relevant and helpful today as it was then."

Wayne Cone, Pastor of Pastoral Care, Cypress Bible Church

"This was the best course our seminary has ever had. It was a lot of fun and the students really participated."

Dr. S., a professor at a Jordanian Seminary

"These workshops are a key feature of our leadership development architecture. The practical biblical foundation, skill orientation and adult learning approach are a powerful combination. We believe in these workshops. That's why we've trained a global network of facilitators."

Dr. Ben Sells, former director, International Center for Excellence in Leadership

"I'm working on my doctorate in marriage and family therapy. I have yet to experience anything in my classes that has helped me personally or in my work with people any more than this training."

Dave, missionary and doctoral student

"I am 72 and have served God for over twenty-five years and I have never had training like this. The way you give it to us is wonderful."

An Egyptian leader

"Think of how many more people will be won to the kingdom because of this workshop! Satan was pushed back with this workshop and glory came to the Lord in the heavenlies—and will come on earth as these folks follow up on these new relationships."

A missionary to Muslims

"The unanimous expression was, 'Why haven't we been presented with this material before?'"

—*Orman Gwynn, missionary in Costa Rica with International Mission Board*

"Thanks for your work for the kingdom. Here's one youth pastor who will use this for change around him. I'm going to be different, not overnight but over the long haul. Here was a workshop that was not hype, emotions and fluff, but nuts and bolts, hammer and trowel foundational stuff! It needs to be a slow-drip learning for lifelong change."

John, youth pastor in Houston, TX

"This workshop is the practical application of walking in the Spirit. I want all the people in my area to have this training by the end of the year!"

A national leader in Kazakhstan

"A simple increase in knowledge about relationships isn't enough to change behavior. Practice is the key and practice is at the core of this workshop. This material applies to every area of my life!"

John, human resources director of a large mission organization

"The workshop helped me see the importance of relationship with others at work and home. If I had gone through this before, it would have saved me a lot of sorrow, pain and sleepless nights in dealing with relationships. I'm a better husband, leader and team member because of this workshop."

Doug, missionary in Surinam

"God moved in a beautiful way on Guam. There were many strained relationships and lack of trust among the staff, but as the topics were dealt with, the Holy Spirit moved in the hearts of the people in a beautiful way. People were going to one another seeking to work through their differences and build relationship not just among the staff, but also in marriages and families."

Peter, missionary in Guam

"This past year was a tough one, but this week was a refreshing gift from God!"

Cyndi, ministry leader in Houston

"This is the only seminar/workshop I have ever come home from feeling like I could do what they taught because I had done it. A very strong spiritual quality permeated everything we did."

Bartel Morgan, Cypress Bible Church, Houston

"My life has been changed. I want to be trained as a facilitator so I can train Arabs all over the Middle East."

A Jordanian leader

"This training should be given to every new Christian in my country."

A leader in Nepal

"I must say it was the best workshop I've ever attended. It has transformed parts of my own personal life. I believe it will be extremely helpful not only for me personally but also for the ministry I'm involved in. The written material is marvelous. Thanks a lot for providing this workshop."

A ministry leader in Nairobi, Kenya

"The workshop has made a difference in my own life. It led me to self-examination and to return to God's gracious mercy and power. God bless you."

A missionary in Argentina

"This workshop is the practical application of walking in the Spirit. I want all the people in my area to have this training by the end of the year!"

A national leader in Kazakhstan

"I came here thinking this was going to help me 'on the job' but throughout the week it became more and more obvious that all of this applies to how I interact as a wife and mom! Like it said on one of the last pages: if you don't practice this at home, don't export it outside the home! It was like attending a marriage-building seminar—without my spouse!"

Karen, a missionary in Kenya

"I came home refreshed, inspired and ready to love anyone and everyone."

Lee Ann, mother and ministry leader in Houston

The Toolbox for Effective Missionaries
Equpping missionaries to change lives for the Kingdom

by Ken Williams, PhD and Gaylyn Williams

The following books are in this series:

Never Do Fundraising Again: You Really Can Transform Donors into Lifelong Partners

Never Fear Conflict Again: How to leverage conflict into intimacy

Stress Busters for Missionaries: You Really Can Balance Your Life and Reclaim Your Sanity

Boost Your Relationship IQ: 7 Skills to Transform Relationships and Build Healthier Communities

More Resources

Go to www.RelationshipResources.org/resources-for-missionaries for more information about:

- Free ebooks and other free materials, including 52 free stress-management tips
- Online courses and workshops, based on the materials in these books
- Discounts on all our books
- Customized books for your mission

This book, formerly called *Reconcilable Differences,* has been customized for missionaries. Some of the materials in this book were first published in *Sharpening Your Interpersonal Skills.*

Other books by the authors include:

Keys to Joy: How to Unlock God's Gift of Lasting Happiness

Sharpening Your Interpersonal Skills

Plus   earlier   versions   of   the   books   in   this   series

Other books by Gaylyn include:

Breakthrough Strategies for Every Believer: A Biblical Guide to Spiritual Warfare

The Surprising Joy of Exploring God's Heart: A Daily Adventure with 365 of His Names

The Surprising Joy of Discovering How God Sees You: A Daily Adventure with Your Identity in Christ

The Surprising Joy of Embracing God's Promises: 365 Reminders of His Faithfulness

2031 Names of God: Transform Your Life as You Get to Know God in New Ways

Overflowing Hope: 31 Devotional Studies to Encourage You

Overflowing Hope for Singles: 31 Devotional Studies to Encourage You

Learn More about these books at www.RelationshipResources.org

Foreword

Life in Christ's church is life lived in relationships with other people. Some are close and personal, some are not—but all require an amazing assortment of skills if those relationships are to be a vital and positive reflection of Jesus Christ. There is no mission group, no missionary, no church, no pastor and no Bible study group that would not profit immensely from this book.

From a solidly biblical platform, it takes a clear and practical look at the major areas that are so critical to any healthy relationship. I have attended my share of "pastor's conferences" and "how-to sessions" designed to improve various facets of my ministry.

Rarely have I been able to say that what I took away was something I use every single day. However, the tools given at the workshop using these materials are truly *everyday* tools. I use them in every relationship—from the casual acquaintance to the most intense counseling situation.

If the opportunity comes your way to attend a Relationship Resources workshop or host one at your church, do not pass it up! You will be making an investment that guarantees a rich return of healthy, Christ-reflecting relationships.

Under His Mercy,

Pastor Tim Westcott

Idyllwild Bible Church, Idyllwild, California

Acknowledgments

I would like to say a special thank you to the following people. Without them, this book would not be possible.

My father, Ken Williams. I'm grateful for all the research he did to make this book possible. It is based on a previous work we did. I miss him and look forward to the day I'll see him again!

My sons, Jonathan and Timothy Whalin. As a single mom, I had many opportunities to practice and refine my interpersonal skills. Thank you for your love and patience with me as I have spent hours researching, writing and practicing these skills with you. Thank you for accepting me and loving me even when I failed to apply these principles with you.

Thank you to each person who proofed or edited this book: Lyndell Martin, John Rodwick, Mark Adams, Jill Miller, Robin Miller, Carol Voisine and Colleen Shine. Thank you to Rubin Paxton, who did so many little, and not-so-little, projects to help make this book a success. Special thanks to Linda Harris with PerfectWordEditing.com for her final edits.

Again, thank you to Gordon and Dian. I wrote and edited much of this book at your lovely cabin, where I find so much inspiration.

Blessings,

Gaylyn

Table of Contents

Introduction

Imitate God, therefore, in everything you do,
because you are his dear children.
Live a life filled with love, following the example of Christ.
He loved us and offered himself as a sacrifice for us,
a pleasing aroma to God.
Ephesians 5:1–2 NLT

Life is a journey—it's easy at times, but other times we face obstacles we must overcome.

Before my son Jonathan went to China as a missionary, we decided to hike Pikes Peak. We camped at its base next to a babbling creek. When it was bitterly cold the next morning, we nestled in our warm sleeping bags longer than planned. After breakfast, we began our journey equipped with water, snacks, sunscreen and other provisions.

After passing timberline, we trudged across Devil's Playground, so named because lighting dances from boulder to boulder around that area. When dark clouds and rumbling thunder moved closer, we turned and rapidly retreated down the rugged trail toward our camp. The next day we made it to the top, although we hitched a ride the last few miles because, once again, dark clouds closed in.

Just as Jonathan and I experienced struggles on our adventure, unexpected conflicts arise in our journeys through relationships. They can either destroy or enhance our relationships. We need to be prepared for whatever happens. Often we need help to get through our conflicts in interactions. This book can be that resource for you, preparing you for any obstacles you may navigate on your relational voyage.

We live in a variety of communities, including family, church, mission, team and more. How we relate to one another will demonstrate whether we are living in ways that glorify God. One of our goals should be to interact with people so they will be drawn to God, us and our communities.

This book builds on *Boost Your Relationship IQ.*[1] If you haven't studied that book yet, I encourage you to take the time to do it first. In that one, we looked at some of the things people do that damage relationships, as well as how to build relationships by listening well, encouraging others, building trust and drawing them out. It is impossible to deal with conflict effectively without having good listening skills. Many people believe they are good at listening, yet very few are.

My dad, Ken Williams, PhD, and I published a book in 1998, *Sharpening Your Interpersonal Skills,* for missionaries. This book is based on and expands on the skills taught in that one. He did research for that book in his doctoral studies on human behavior as well as many years of counseling and training mission leaders worldwide. I've added much to our original work. My father went home to be with Jesus in April 2013.

This book contains practical skills to transform your communities through learning skills to effectively manage conflict. Although building new patterns in our lives is not always easy, it is worth it.[2] We have seen entire ministries changed as they learned and used these skills.

Congratulations. You have taken the first and vital step toward living out God's Word in your relationships by studying this book. You'll discover practical biblical keys to guide you on your journey through conflict. I pray that as you continue your lifelong journey you will be abundantly blessed by the Lord.

Blessings,

Gaylyn

Gaylyn Williams, President of Relationship Resources

Note:
- For simplicity, masculine forms are used to designate both genders.
- Some verses are used many times because they fit into more than one context.
- Most people's names and some details from the stories have been changed to protect the innocent and not-so-innocent.

---

[1] You can learn more about the process of building new patterns in the Appendix.

Benefits from this Study

You can benefit from this study in the following ways:
- Cultivate strong communities that glorify God and draw people to Him and to your group—both believers and not-yet believers
- Deepen your personal knowledge of the Bible
- Grow in your relationship with God
- Learn how to live out God's Word in all your relationships
- Discover step-by-step, practical applications to enrich your life
- Develop effective communication expertise to deepen your connections
- Discern what others are communicating to you, both verbally and nonverbally
- Challenge your personal and community core beliefs
- Build rapport with others quickly, to enhance your interactions and communication
- Create receptivity to your ideas
- Establish a bond of trust resulting in long-term, meaningful associations
- Break free of your fears and the security of your comfort zone, pushing you beyond whatever hinders your relationships[3]

How Is this Book Different?

The principles in this book have been tested and proven with about forty-thousand people worldwide for over forty years. In this book we look at biblical principles that are critical for our lives and relationships. I challenge you not only to read what is here but to put each part into practice.

Everything in this book is based on understanding and applying God's Word to relationships. It is the basis for all relationships and communication. It has so much to say about how we are to interact toward those around us.

The verses at the beginning of the introduction are foundational to the principles taught in this book. We are commanded to imitate God. What an incredible order! It would be completely impossible if we were not His cherished children. Since God is love, the best way we can imitate Him is to treat people as He did. We'll look at this more in Chapter 1.

---

3 Learn more about comfort zones in the Appendix.

This is an interactive workbook designed to help you effectively communicate with everyone in your life. It contains thoroughly road-tested, step-by-step biblical skills and learning methods to enrich your spiritual, personal and professional life.

The purpose of this book is to give you practical biblical direction so you can be victorious in your life and your communities. It will help you grow in how you relate to others in your attitudes, knowledge and skills, equipping you with the ability to build strong relationships.

People skills are essential in every area of our lives with—family, friends, coworkers, boss, fellow believers as well as not-yet believers.

What This Book Includes

This book is divided into six Keys to unlock relationships:

1. *Embrace Conflict as an Ally* unlocks the keys to effectively managing conflict to build your relationships, rather than destroying them.
2. *To Err is Human*—to Confront Is Divine unlocks keys to make confrontation positive, rather than negative.
3. *Ticking Time Bombs* unlocks skills to lower anger with someone attacking you verbally so you can come to a win/win situation.
4. *Facilitate Peace* unlocks skills to empower others to manage their conflicts.
5. *Houston, We Have a Problem* unlocks seven powerful steps to help you or others find solutions to problems.
6. *Overcome Obstacles* solidifies the unlocked skills.

Each section examines a key skill you can apply to relationships with anyone in your communities—family members, friends, colleagues and even acquaintances. As you complete the activities, your communication skills and knowledge of Scripture will be strengthened.

Each Key is Divided into Three to Four Chapters

- The first one or two chapters under each Key provide a big-picture overview of the concept. Discover a deeper understanding of real-life, practical information focused on critical concepts, grounded in the Word.
- The following chapter, is a reality check, with self-assessment tools to identify current skills. You'll evaluate how effective you are at using your newly acquired abilities with your family as well as others.
- The final chapter in each section is an opportunity to practice what you've learned. It provides practical tips and tools for improvements.

Most of the skills are demonstrated in videos that you will have access to online, so you can see how to do—or not do—the skill.

Each Key Also Includes the Following

Scriptures: Dig into God's Word to unearth what God says about the topic. Reinforce each skill with scriptural principles.

Powerful Stories: Through their personal stories, learn how others applied the key principles.

Activities: Integrate God's Word, knowledge and abilities to effectively apply them in your personal and professional life.

Case Studies: Consider real-life situations to emphasize effective responses and communication.

Questions for Personal or Group Study: Dig deeper personally or with others through thought-provoking questions and Bible studies.

Strategies for Success: Write a brief account of past or current situations. Evaluate how you did and anything you may do differently as a result of this study.

Snapshots: Record specific issues you want to practice and master. As you finish each chapter, go to the "Snapshots" page at the back of this book. Write one or two things you specifically want to remember from that section. This will serve as a reminder of the areas where you desire growth.

On any of these, you may want to have a journal to answer the questions, especially if you need more room. I personally use Evernote as a journal. I use it on my smart phone, tablet, laptop or desktop to record my journal entries, making it available on all the devices.

How to Use this Book

You can use this book in any of the following ways, or you can get creative in how you use it.

- If you use this book with others, you can help each other along the path and pray for each other.
- If you are studying the book with others, look at the "Leaders' Guide" in the back of this book for some helpful ideas.
- As you study this book, hold your expectations in an open hand to the Lord, allowing God to do whatever He wants to do in your life

during this study. Trust Him to reveal His plans for you and bring them to reality.

Study It Alone

- Make a commitment to seriously study and grow in each skill.
- Find a partner for accountability.
- For the most benefit, complete all assignments. If you need extra space to answer questions, use a separate page or a journal.
- Decide not to let urgent things in your life crowd out time for study.

Study with Your Spouse, a Friend, Your Children or Teens

- Read it separately and then share the principles.
- Or read it together and talk about what you are learning.
- Pray for each other as you learn to apply the skills.
- Study it with your children or teens, empowering them with the tools they need for strong relationships.

Study with a Small Group, Your Whole Church or Mission

You can use this with a small group, or your whole mission, learning and applying the principles together. You could do one Key a week. Here are some ideas that can help you:
- Use the suggestions above.
- Read through the suggestions for small groups in the Appendix[4].
- Interact with others
  - o to gain more insight;
  - o to develop and practice interpersonal skills;

  - o to learn about your issues of growth;
  - o to minister to one another and to be ministered to.

Attend a Workshop

To attend or set up a workshop for your group, contact Relationship Resources.[5]

Take This Course Online

---

4 Contact us about leader's materials. at info@RelationshipResources.org.
5 Email us at Info@RelationshipResources.org.

You'll be able to interact with others who are taking it. [6]

Other Information That Might Be Helpful

When I mention other books I've written, they are all available on Amazon or www.RelationshipResources.org. You can also learn more about them at the back of this book.

Meditation

Meditation has received a bad reputation with Christians because of the way other religions use it. However, the Bible has a lot to say about meditation. Look up the following verses. Think about what each one says about meditating on God and His Word.

Joshua 1:8 (NKJV): "This Book of the Law shall not depart from your mouth, but you shall meditate in it day and night, that you may observe to do according to all that is written in it. For then you will make your way prosperous, and then you will have good success."

Psalm 1:1–2 (HCSB): "How happy is the man who does not follow the advice of the wicked, or take the path of sinners, or join a group of mockers! Instead, his delight is in the LORD's instruction, and he meditates on it day and night."

Psalm 48:9 (NIV): "Within your temple, O God, we meditate on your unfailing love."

Psalm 77:12 (ESV): "I will ponder all your work, and meditate on your mighty deeds." The *New Living Translation* says, "They are constantly in my thoughts. I cannot stop thinking about your mighty works."

Psalm 119:27 (NLT): "Help me understand the meaning of your commandments, and I will meditate on your wonderful deeds."

Psalm 119:97, 99 (ASV): "Oh how I love thy law! It is my meditation all the day. … I have more understanding than all my teachers; for thy testimonies are my meditation."

Psalm 145:5 (NKJV): "I will meditate on the glorious splendor of Your majesty, and on Your wondrous works."

Philippians 4:8 (ESV): "Whatever is true, whatever is honorable, whatever is just, whatever is pure, whatever is lovely, whatever is commendable, if

---

6 Go to www.RRcourses.com to learn more.

there is any excellence, if there is anything worthy of praise, think about these things."

Other synonyms for meditate include consider, think about, study, contemplate, ponder, deliberate, examine and mull over.

I encourage you to take the time to meditate on and consider the truths throughout this book. Ask the Lord to reveal His truth to you as you meditate on His Word.

Scripture Memory

In each chapter, I encourage you to memorize Bible verses. When you have the Word in your heart, you'll be amazed at the times God brings it back to you—just when you need it. I've been memorizing Scripture since I was a child. Often during the night, if I can't sleep, I'll meditate on a verse. For help on memorizing verses, go to my blog www.DailyNameofGod.com.

Bible Translations

This book uses different translations of the Bible, which show variations and nuances of the verses. Only parts of some verses are used, because that is what is being emphasized. The copyright information for the Bible translations is on the copyright page at the end of this book.

The abbreviations used are:

AMP—Amplified Bible

ASV—American Standard Version

CEV—Contemporary English Version

CJB—Complete Jewish Bible

ESV—English Standard Version

GW—God's Word

HCSB—Holman Christian Standard Bible

NASB—New American Standard Bible

NET—The NET Bible

NIV—New International Version

NJB—New Jerusalem Bible

NKJV—New King James Version

NLT—New Living Translation

RSV—Revised Standard Version

Formatting for Verses

I don't change anything within the verses, but quote them exactly as they are in the translation I'm using, with the exception of omitting words that are not essential for the topic. For example, if one translation capitalizes pronouns for God and another doesn't, I use whatever the translation does. Or if a translation uses a different spelling than United States standards, I leave the word as it is. If something is not obvious in the verse, but is known from the context, I might include that in brackets.

Chapter 1

All You Need is Love

Jesus replied, "'You must love the Lord your God
with all your heart, all your soul, and all your mind.'
This is the first and greatest commandment.
A second is equally important: 'Love your neighbor as yourself.'
The entire law and all the demands of the prophets
are based on these two commandments."
Matthew 22:37–40 NLT

I grew up knowing my earthly father loved me, however he and my mom left me at boarding school from the time I was six years old to thirteen, with only getting to see my family for vacations. As a consequence, I subconsciously wondered if God would also abandon me. I figured, if my human parents would do that, God probably would as well. My parents were missionaries in a remote village high in the mountains of Guatemala. As an adult, I now understand that boarding school was their only option; however, as a child, it felt like I was abandoned.

As a child, it seemed that my parents had *more important* things to do, like serving God (I was told this numerous times by the teachers at the boarding school.) I was sure Father God also had more important things to do than listen to me or help me. It has been a challenge growing to grasp God's love for me. I know I will continue growing in it for the rest of my life, because His love is so much deeper than I can begin to imagine.

Many of us have struggled to view God as loving because of how our parents treated us. If they, especially our fathers, were unloving, we may assume that our Father in Heaven is also unloving. Does this resonate with you or someone you know? You may need time to consider how you view your heavenly Father.

Before we can effectively manage conflict with others, we need to understand how much God loves us. The more we recognize His love for us, the more we fall in love with Him. Then we can allow His love to flow through us to others—especially those with whom we struggle. When we comprehend and experience God's love, we are able to respond to conflict in God-honoring ways.

I encourage you to take time to study what the Word has to say about God's love. Ask Him to reveal how much He cares about you in ways you can comprehend. You may need to ask Him to heal places of hurt and brokenness from your past, before you can fully grasp His love. To do that, you may want to go through inner healing, as I have.[1]

Let's Start at the Beginning

God created us in His image. Genesis 1:27 (CJB) says, "God created humankind in his own image; in the image of God he created him: male and female he created them."

What does it mean to be created in God's image? Does this mean our bodies are the same as His? The Bible talks about God's arms, hands, legs, eyes, ears, heart and more. That is part of how He created us.

Who is God? What is He like? As you read through the Bible, you'll find His different characteristics. In my book, *2031 Names of God*, I reveal many of them through His names.

I believe God's primary quality is love. That is the bottom line of His character. First John 4:16 (NLT) tells us that God is love. "We know how much God loves us, and we have put our trust in his love. God is love, and all who live in love live in God, and God lives in them."

Adam and Eve lived in a perfect environment, including intimacy with God, until they sinned. At that point, sin entered the world, affecting all mankind.

Because God is holy, He could no longer allow people to live in His presence, unless blood sacrifices were offered to cover sins. Hebrews 9:22 (ESV) says, "Without the shedding of blood there is no forgiveness of sins." In the Old Testament the people had to continually offer sacrifices to pay for their sins.

---

1 To find someone who does inner healing, ask at your church, your mission or search the internet for "inner healing" and your city. Some types of inner healing include Sozo, Healing Prayer, Soaking Prayer and Theophostic. Make sure whatever you choose is biblically based and not New Age.

God longed for a relationship with us that would last forever; so He sent His beloved, sinless Son as a once-for-all sacrifice for our sins. Jesus paid that price, so that all who believe in Him can have a relationship with Him both now and for eternity.

Meditate on what these verses say about what God did to show how much He loves you:

John 3:16 (ESV): "God so loved the world, that he gave his only Son, that whoever believes in him should not perish but have eternal life."

Ephesians 2:4–5 (NIV): "Because of his great love for us, God, who is rich in mercy, made us alive with Christ even when we were dead in transgressions—it is by grace you have been saved."

1 John 2:1–2 (NIV): "My dear children, I write this to you so that you will not sin. But if anybody does sin, we have an advocate with the Father— Jesus Christ, the Righteous One. He is the atoning sacrifice for our sins, and not only for ours but also for the sins of the whole world."

1 John 4:9–10 (NLT): "God showed how much he loved us by sending his one and only Son into the world so that we might have eternal life through him. This is real love—not that we loved God, but that he loved us and sent his Son as a sacrifice to take away our sins."

Jesus was willing to take on your sins, sacrificing His life so you could have eternal life with Him. Take time to meditate on these amazing facts. What does it mean to you that God loves you so much He was willing to give His precious Son's life for you?

Imagine

Consider how God *might* have made the decision to show His love to us. I'm not saying this is what happened. However, here is a possible scenario of what might have occurred in Heaven, before Earth was created. Read this with an open mind, asking God to show you how much it cost Him to reveal His love to you.

Imagine this: the Father, Jesus and Holy Spirit are talking about their incredible relationship and how much they love each other. Yet they want to bring others into their family. They discuss various ways to do that, including creating Earth with perfect humans who would love them. However, they know that people can only truly be devoted to them, if they have free wills to choose to love or not. God also knows Satan will tempt Adam and Eve, which will bring sin into the entire human race. Because

God is holy, sin would have to be atoned for if people were to have intimacy with Him.

After discussing how to overcome the gulf that sin would put between God and man, Jesus offers to go to Earth to pay the penalty for everyone's sins. At first, the Father and Holy Spirit totally reject the idea. They can't bear the thought of allowing the sinless Son of God to take on all the sins of the world to save people who will hate God.

They know sending Jesus to Earth is the only way to have a long-term relationship with mankind. But first they decide to give laws people must keep and sacrifices to pay for their own sins. This is necessary so people can see how the holy God can't tolerate sin. Then when Jesus pays the ultimate sacrifice, people hopefully will begin to comprehend how much it cost and how much God loves them.

Eventually they agree that Jesus, going to earth as a sinless sacrifice, is the only way to increase their family. They want to show their unfailing love to all these new children and receive their affection in return. Thus begins the most incredible love story ever told.

Now think about when Jesus was on earth. Often we focus on how much He suffered for us—as we should. However, consider how difficult it must have been for the Father and Holy Spirit to watch Jesus be rejected, betrayed, hated and crucified. Imagine them wanting to stop Jesus' pain, yet knowing if they stepped in, we could never enter into their family, giving and receiving love.

Think about how much it cost:

- Jesus, God's only Son, to die for us, paying the cost for our sins, so we could become God's beloved children.
- Father God to not only allow Jesus to suffer and die, but also to *give* Him to die (John 3:16).
- The Holy Spirit, knowing He had the power to stop Jesus' pain, but also recognizing He couldn't stop it, otherwise we could not have a relationship with God.

We don't know how God decided on the plan to save us, but I highly doubt it was easy for any of them—Jesus, Father God or the Holy Spirit. What does it mean to you seeing all they endured to make you a part of their loving family? Take some time to thank God for what He did to reveal His love for you.

God's Love for His People:

Throughout the Bible we see God's love for His people. First, let's look at a few verses in the Old Testament. What do they say to you?

Exodus 34:6 (NET): "The LORD, the LORD, the compassionate and gracious God, slow to anger, and abounding in loyal love and faithfulness."

Deuteronomy 7:9 (ESV): "Know therefore that the LORD your God is God, the faithful God who keeps covenant and steadfast love with those who love him and keep his commandments, to a thousand generations."

Psalm 5:7 (NASB): "By Your abundant lovingkindness I will enter Your house, at Your holy temple I will bow in reverence for You."

Psalm 13:5 (NLT): "I trust in your unfailing love. I will rejoice because you have rescued me."

Psalm 36:7 (HCSB) "God, Your faithful love is so valuable that people take refuge in the shadow of Your wings."

Psalm 40:11 (NLT): "LORD, don't hold back your tender mercies from me. Let your unfailing love and faithfulness always protect me."

Psalm 57:10 (ESV): "Your steadfast love is great to the heavens, your faithfulness to the clouds."

Psalm 89:2 (RSV): "Thy steadfast love was established for ever, thy faithfulness is firm as the heavens."

Psalm 119:64 (NJB): "Your faithful love fills the earth, Yahweh."

Psalm 145:8 (ESV): "The LORD is gracious and merciful, slow to anger and abounding in steadfast love."

We can have a relationship with God because of His great love for us. That is amazing good news! Now, read a powerful New Testament passage about what God did for us and how much He loves us. Then answer the questions following it.

Romans 8:32–39 (ESV): "He who did not spare his own Son but gave him up for us all, how will he not also with him graciously give us all things? 33 Who shall bring any charge against God's elect? It is God who justifies. 34 Who is to condemn? Christ Jesus is the one who died— more than that, who was raised—who is at the right hand of God, who indeed is interceding for us. 35 Who shall separate us from the love of Christ? Shall tribulation, or distress, or persecution, or famine, or nakedness, or danger, or sword? [36] As it is written, 'For your sake we are being killed all the day long; we are regarded as sheep to be slaughtered.' [37] No, in all these things we are more than conquerors through him who loved us. [38] For I am sure that neither death nor life, nor angels nor rulers, nor things present nor things to come, nor powers, [39] nor height nor depth, nor anything else in all creation, will be able to separate us from the love of God in Christ Jesus our Lord."

1. What can you learn about God's love for you from this passage?

2. What does it mean to you that Father God would give His beloved Son's life for you?

3. Consider this: since God gave His most precious possession for you, is there anything that He wouldn't do for you?

4. What is Jesus doing for you right now? (verse 34)

5. What can separate you from God's love? (verses 35, 38–39)

6. Do you really believe the truths in these verses? Why or why not? If you don't, what is keeping you from believing them?

7. Ask God to reveal a new level of His love for you from these verses.

You Are God's Loved Child

What do these verses say about being God's child?

John 1:12 (NKJV): "As many as received Him, to them He gave the right to become children of God, to those who believe in His name."

Romans 8:16 (ESV): "The Spirit himself bears witness with our spirit that we are children of God."

1 John 3:1 (NIV): "See what great love the Father has lavished on us, that we should be called children of God! And that is what we are! The reason the world does not know us is that it did not know him."

Based on the verses you just read, answer these questions:

1. Are you certain you are God's child? Why or why not?

2. What does it mean to you to be a child of God?

3. How did God show you His love? (See 1 John 3:1 above.) What does it look like to lavish love on someone?

4. Think about who your loving Heavenly Father is. He is the King of kings (Revelation 19:16). Is there anything He couldn't give you?

5. Considering what God did to show you His love by sending His own Son to die for you, how do you think He will treat you now?

6. Do you believe you have to beg Him for what you need? Why or why not?

How Does God Show His Love?

God shows us His love in many ways. We'll look at just a few of them. I encourage you to study the Word to discover the myriad of other ways God shows you His love. Ask Him to reveal what He wants you to know through these verses:

He protects: 1 Peter 1:5 (NLT): "Through your faith, God is protecting you by his power until you receive this salvation, which is ready to be revealed on the last day for all to see."

He gives strength: Philippians 4:13 (NIV): "I can do all this through him who gives me strength."

He provides for all your needs: Philippians 4:19 (NIV): "My God will meet all your needs according to the riches of his glory in Christ Jesus."

He gives mercy, hope and an inheritance: 1 Peter 1:3–4 (ESV): "Blessed be the God and Father of our Lord Jesus Christ! According to his great mercy, he has caused us to be born again to a living hope through the resurrection of Jesus Christ from the dead, to an inheritance that is imperishable, undefiled, and unfading, kept in heaven for you."

He gives everything you need for life and godliness: 2 Peter 1:3 (GW): "God's divine power has given us everything we need for life and for godliness. This power was given to us through knowledge of the one who called us by his own glory and integrity."

He *sozos* you. Luke 19:10 (NLT): "The Son of Man came to seek and save those who are lost." The Greek word for "save" is *sozo*, meaning so much more than just to save. It also means He heals, delivers, makes us whole, protects and preserves us. Meditate on all that Jesus did and does for you.

Think about how else God shows you His love. There are dozens of ways, possibly hundreds! I encourage you to read the Bible searching for how God reveals His love.

What Does God Want from Us?

The verses at the beginning of this chapter reveal what God requires of us. In Matthew 22:37–40 (NLT) Jesus says, "'You must love the Lord your God with all your heart, all your soul, and all your mind.' This is the first and greatest commandment. A second is equally important: 'Love your neighbor as yourself.' The entire law and all the demands of the prophets are based on these two commandments."

Let's break these verses down. We are to do the following:
1. **Love God.** We are to love the Lord our God with our whole being—with all our hearts, souls and minds.
2. **Love our neighbor as ourselves.** We can't love our neighbor until we love ourselves.

3. **Love ourselves**. What do you think that means? I believe at least part of it is seeing ourselves as God see us—through His eyes. God loves you just as you are, with all your faults and failures. He accepts you just as you are, but He loves you so much that He wants to help you become His strong, loving and confident child.

   The first step to loving yourself is accepting how much God loves you. What holds you back from accepting God's love for you and loving yourself?

I have so much delight in my first grandchild, Samuel. He brings me great joy. Do you think I get angry with him and punish him when he cries or dirties his diaper? Of course not. I accept him for where he is. However, if he is still soiling his diaper when he is thirty years old, he may need some help! In the same way, our Heavenly Father loves us and accepts us just the way we are.

When Samuel gets a little older, how do you think I'll react when he asks me for anything he needs (not necessarily for all of his *wants*)? Will he have to beg and plead with me? No, if it is in my ability (and his parents approve), I will freely give him anything he needs.

Your Heavenly Father cares for you even more than I love my grandson. He will freely give you everything you need—and you never have to beg Him. Think about that.

What Is the Result of Understanding God's Love?

When we fully comprehend how much God loves us, we are empowered to love each other. What do these verses tell you?

1 John 4:11 (NLT): "Dear friends, since God loved us that much, we surely ought to love each other."

1 John 3:16 (NIV): "This is how we know what love is: Jesus Christ laid down his life for us. And we ought to lay down our lives for our brothers and sisters."

Ephesians 5:1–2 (ESV): "Be imitators of God, as beloved children. And walk in love, as Christ loved us and gave himself up for us, a fragrant offering and sacrifice to God."

God's love for us should spill over and out of us onto each person we come in contact with. Then when conflict arises or someone does anything hurtful to us, we know we don't have to respond by getting even or angry.

When we truly recognize how much God loves us and His love is living in us, we see others through His eyes. And we will treat others with His love flowing out of us. When they hurt us we don't have to take it personally. Instead we might feel sad for them since they are acting like they don't understand how much God loves them.

Yes, there will still be times when we must confront others, when they are doing something wrong or hurting someone. But our love will cover a multitude of sins (1 Peter 4:8). We will no longer need to confront everything. We'll be able to bear with others and forgive them, as Christ forgave us (Colossians 3:12–14).[2]

I'm still growing in this. I'm learning to be fully immersed in God's love for me, to love Him and then to let my relationship with Him spill over onto anyone around me. It's a process that has been such an incredible journey.

A young woman backed into my car in a gas station, crunching my bumper. We exchanged information and I talked to her insurance company, only to find out her insurance had lapsed. She was willing to pay over time for the hundreds of dollars of damage. After praying about what to do, the Lord told me to forgive her debt to fix my car and tell her about God's forgiveness for her. I called her to tell her she didn't need to pay me. Then I shared about God's love and forgiveness. I encouraged her to read her dusty Bible to learn more about God. She was open to learning about God, because she could see I demonstrated forgiveness to her.

Two Examples

Here are two examples of people who live out of their love with God and let it spill over to every person around them.

Heidi Baker is a missionary in Mozambique with her husband, Rolland. She comprehends how loved she is and it spills out all over everyone she encounters. She and her husband set up a network of over ten thousand churches, feed over ten thousand children daily and much more. Everything they do demonstrates God's love. If you have an opportunity, watch *Compelled by Love*, the movie made of her life. I had the privilege of living in Mozambique and sitting under her teaching for a month and a half. I watched her treat everyone with the same love, whether an "important" person from the United States or a beggar child with bare feet.

Dan Mohler is a pastor who is so much in love with God because He recognizes how much God loves him. He says, "You can't hurt me, because

---

2 *Boost Your Relationship IQ* has a whole chapter on forgiving and bearing with others.

I know who I am." He understands that he is a cherished child of God. If people say or do anything mean or unkind, rather than feeling hurt he feels sorry for them. He recognizes they act as they do because they don't accept how much God loves them. Consequently, joy radiates from his life. I encourage you to watch some of his videos on YouTube. They are transformational.

Before we can begin to handle conflict effectively with others, we must first acknowledge how much God loves us. When we know how much He loves us, we'll fall more in love with Him. And our love relationship with God will spill all over those we encounter—both believers and not-yet-believers.

The rest of this course reveals specific ways to handle conflict, all based on this solid foundation. Without it, all our efforts to solve conflict will be just that—our efforts. They will be futile. But when we consider God's abounding love for us, then we can do all things with His love that flows through us to others.

Questions for Personal or Group Study

Consider the following alone or with a group:

1. Review this chapter.

    a. What stands out for you?

    b. Write down any areas in which you need to improve. What will you do to grow in each area?

    c. Look back over all the verses in this chapter. Pick some to meditate on and memorize. You might want to write them on cards or sticky notes and put them where you'll see them often.

2. How have you experienced God's love for you?

3. What keeps you from fully experiencing it?

4. How does God's love affect your life and relationships?

5. How might understanding God's love more fully do the following?

    a. Help you love others better, especially those you have a hard time loving, because of conflict

    b. Empower you to effectively manage conflict

6. Make a commitment to read the Bible every day to discover God's love for you in greater ways. Ask Him to fill you with a deeper appreciation of His love for you so it spills over to everyone you encounter.

A Verse to Meditate On and Memorize

Choose a verse from this chapter. If you are not sure which to choose, try one of these passages:

Ephesians 5:1–2 (ESV): "Be imitators of God, as beloved children. And walk in love, as Christ loved us and gave himself up for us, a fragrant offering and sacrifice to God."

Matthew 22:37–40 (NLT): Jesus said, "'You must love the Lord your God with all your heart, all your soul, and all your mind.' This is the first and greatest commandment. A second is equally important: 'Love your neighbor as yourself.' The entire law and all the demands of the prophets are based on these two commandments."

Snapshots

Go to the section titled "Snapshots" to record points you want to remember and/or do.

Key #1: Embrace Conflict as Your Ally

Conflict is inevitable anywhere there are people—with family and friends, at church, in your community and in your mission. It can either devastate or strengthen relationships. Proven biblical principles guide churches, ministries, missions businesses and individuals to transform conflict into strong, God-honoring relationships. These principles apply to any relationship: marriage and family, teams, congregations, coworkers, friends and others.

Conflict is often seen as an enemy, yet it can become an ally if we understand it and follow a few simple principles. It can strengthen and enhance relationships when it is managed in healthy ways. Depending on the degree to which we are able to successfully embrace conflict as an ally, we'll develop healthier, stronger relationships.

This Key provides a foundation for the rest of the book with a basic strategy to manage any conflict. In the other Keys, we'll examine specific types of conflict.

Managing conflict well requires good listening skills. If you haven't studied *Boost Your Relationship IQ*, I suggest you study that course first. It provides foundational principles for this course and emphasizes the importance of listening skills.

Chapter 2

Conflict Is Inevitable, but Combat Is Optional

How good and pleasant it is when God's people live together in unity!
Psalm 133:1 NIV

The apostle Paul and Barnabas went on one of the most famous mission trips—all around the Middle East. They preached the gospel, saw numerous people saved, established many churches, appointed elders in each church, performed countless signs and wonders and much more. God used them in powerful ways. Barnabas's cousin John Mark [1] joined them, but later abandoned them.

After returning to Antioch, the church that had sent them and spending time there, they began talking about another trip together. Barnabas wanted to take John Mark with them, but Paul didn't because he had deserted them before. These godly men, who each served God faithfully, had a major conflict—such a "sharp disagreement that they parted company" (Acts 15:39).[2]

If even the great apostle Paul and Barnabas had a major conflict they couldn't resolve other than going their separate ways, we shouldn't be surprised when we experience conflict.

Conflict is normal in relationships. Living and/or working closely together over time means that we will surely disagree occasionally, and we will probably offend and irritate each other. We have different personalities, backgrounds, tastes, lifestyles and needs. These differences often result in conflicts. Accepting conflict as a fact of life helps us deal with it better.

---

1 Colossians 4:10.

2 See Acts 13-15 for more about this situation.

Do definitions of conflict lead you to believe that all conflict is bad? Conflicts are not destructive in themselves. *The way we handle them* determines how destructive they are. In fact, when we handle conflicts well, we tend to draw closer to each other.

I have a confession to make. I really don't like dealing with conflict. I'd rather we would all get along. I'd prefer to give in to others than to address conflict. Can you relate? However, I've learned that, in order to have God-honoring relationships, I need to deal with conflict in positive ways that build the relationship and community.

Conflict is an inescapable fact of life—even if we choose to run from it or ignore it. It has many possible causes. We may react when something important is threatened, such as

- ideas;
- values;
- goals;
- successes;
- relationships.

What are other causes of conflict you've seen?

This chapter provides a strategy to help you grow in all your relationships by overcoming conflict. You can apply the principles and ground rules even if the other person is unaware of the concepts presented or unwilling to follow them.

The approach in this chapter can be freeing. It offers the following advantages, helping you to

- slow down and work on disagreements step-by-step;
- disconnect from the other person's anger;
- reduce inappropriate expressions of feelings;
- improve relationships in potentially dramatic ways;
- learn how to validate what the other person is feeling;
- focus on productive responses.

Our effectiveness in serving God depends on how well we relate to others and we can only experience healthy, close relationships as we manage our conflicts well.

Reflect on the following and write your thoughts:

1. How do you typically respond to conflict with someone?

2. What conflicts have you had or can you foresee with any or all of these groups of people?

    - spouse or close friend

    - children or other family members

    - people in your church or mission

    - coworkers, team or bosses

3. Have you ever utilized these typical—but unsuccessful—methods to cope with conflict? If so, what was the result?

    - harbor anger inside and refuse to talk with the other person

    - withdraw because you do not like to quarrel

    - allow yourself to get angry, criticize, call names, use sarcasm or act aggressively

    - acquiesce to avoid conflict (possibly say with a big sigh, "You are right.")

    - pretend "everything is okay" when inside you may feel anger or hostility

Conflict is an opportunity for

- constructive change;
- positive growth;
- improved communication;
- better understanding and appreciation for differences.

As we begin our study, we want to lay a firm foundation to help you learn to manage conflict more effectively. Core beliefs are critical to understand for this tudy.

How Core Beliefs Influence Relationships

Your core beliefs, which determine how you live your life, are foundational. Since this concept is so important, this course challenges you to look at your own belief system.

For the purposes of this course, a core belief is defined as *a firmly held conviction that consistently motivates your behavior.*

Belief + Consistent Action = Core Belief

A belief is something you say you believe. However, a core belief is not *only* what you state you believe, but how you act most of the time. Your core beliefs determine much of what you think and feel about life, yourself and others. If you have healthy biblical core beliefs, your relationships will be strong and successful. However, if your core beliefs are not healthy, your relationships will suffer.

Core beliefs regarding communication affect the success or failure of your relationships. As you study, you may discover beliefs that limit your potential to build rewarding personal, professional and spiritual relationships. Ask God to give you an open mind to what He wants to teach you.

Insights about Core Beliefs

- A belief is something you accept as true, but don't necessarily act upon it. A core belief demonstrates how you live, not just what you say you believe. It is foundational to your personality; it becomes the real you.
- You can have ideas you claim to feel strongly about, but if you don't demonstrate them in the way you live, they are merely superficial ways of thinking—not core beliefs.
- The term "believe" in the New Testament usually refers to a core belief—something acted upon. Read James 2:14–26. What do those verses say about the relationship between actions and beliefs?

- You may or may not be aware of your core beliefs. Many beliefs are acted out but not thought out. In other words, you may act on your core beliefs, but you haven't analyzed or acknowledged what you believe.
- "Consistent" does not mean you live them out perfectly. Rather, it means the usual way you live. For example, you may have a conviction about the importance of daily Bible reading. If you read your Bible most days, but occasionally miss a day, you are living that core belief. However, if you only open your Bible on Sundays, this is not a core belief; it is only something you say you believe.
- If your core beliefs accurately reflect truth and reality, they motivate you to act appropriately. The opposite is also true—some may be false and lead you to act inappropriately.

Seven Ways to Determine Your Personal Core Beliefs

Core beliefs are personal, so no one can impose them on you. You don't have to agree with the ones given in this course. Study each one presented, then do the following:

- Consider whether you believe it as it is written.
- Wrestle with where you are in relation to it.
- Ask yourself if you act consistently upon it.
- Evaluate if you want to implement it into your life.
- Make it your own or determine what you want your core belief to be in the area presented.
- Rewrite it to reflect how you live or how you want to live.
- Modify your actions to reflect what you say you believe.

Six Core Beliefs about Managing Conflicts Well

I challenge you to study all of these core beliefs, because they can dramatically affect your relationships.

Core Belief #1

Relationship is almost always more important than the issue!

Some people live as though the issue causing the conflict is almost always more important than the relationship. They make a big deal over every issue, not caring whether they damage their relationships. An example of when the issue may be more important than the relationship is if someone is trying to force you to do something you know is illegal or immoral or someone is abusing you or others. [3]

While this course deals with reconcilable differences, there are some that are *irreconcilable*. You may never come to an agreement; however, in most cases, it is important not to damage the relationship. Instead, you can choose to love the person and agree to disagree on the issue. Some examples include politics, sexual orientation and pro-life/pro-choice. If we break off the relationship with every person we disagree with, we can't have an influence on their lives, potentially bringing them to Christ.

Think about Core Belief #1, then answer these questions:

1. How do you react to this statement?

2. Normally, is the issue more important to you than the relationship? Explain.

3. Can you afford to continue making the issue more important than the relationship? Why or why not?

4. What changes can you make to help your communities?

Core Belief #2

Healthy relationships cannot be built on a 50/50 philosophy.

We must be willing to go *beyond half way in order to support and help each other when needed.*

Think about Core Belief #2 and answer these questions:

1. What does this mean to you in your communities?

---

3 In the Appendix, you'll find a list of Scriptures about when the issue may be more important than the relationship.

2. Do your relationships reflect this core belief? Why or why not?

3. What percentage do you think your relationships are built on? How is that working or not working for you?

4. Based on this core belief, what changes could you make to help your communities?

5. How do these verses help your understanding?

   Galatians 6:2 (NIV): "Carry each other's burdens, and in this way you will fulfill the law of Christ."

   Look at 1 Corinthians 13:1–7 in the "Questions for Personal or Group Study."

This kind of love goes far beyond a 50/50 arrangement. In fact, it doesn't even think about who is giving the most. It says, "I'm willing to go more than half way. When you aren't up to carrying your part of the load because of physical, spiritual or emotional distress, I'll gladly bear your part of the load." When we're able to apply 1 Corinthians 13, there is greater care and security in our relationships because we allow for weaknesses and failures.

Core Belief #3

A commitment to honesty is foundational.

Let's be lovingly honest about our feelings. It's possible to share our feelings clearly and honestly without condemning or blaming others. We must also be honest about how we feel when others are *not causing our feelings*. If we are distressed over something, we need to share it so those around us know how we feel and can respond accordingly.

The other side of honesty is being willing to listen to others' honest expression of feelings even when we may have triggered them. It isn't easy to accept others' feelings, especially when they reveal our failures and weaknesses!

We may have to continually work at keeping walls from being built between us that block open communication. Accepting each other's feelings as valid is part of this process.

Think about Core Belief #3 and answer these questions:

1. How does a commitment to honesty build your relationships in your communities?

2. Are you normally upfront and honest with what you think and feel? Explain.

3. If you are tempted to be dishonest in your ministry or personal life, can you afford to continue acting this way? Why or why not?

4. What could you change to help your relationships?

5. If you don't have a commitment to honesty, consider making that commitment right now.

6. How do these verses help you understand this core belief?

   Ephesians 4:15 (ESV): "Speaking the truth in love, we are to grow up in every way into him who is the head, into Christ." Honesty must be balanced with Christian love.

   Ephesians 4:25 (NLT): "Stop telling lies. Let us tell our neighbors the truth, for we are all parts of the same body." God's command to honesty applies to all relationships. This means being open and transparent to the point of painful vulnerability at times, even if we might be misjudged and misunderstood when we reveal our true feelings.

Core Belief #4

High stress usually lowers our tolerance for conflict.[4]

Intense external and internal stress can seriously hinder our ability to bear with others and to manage conflicts. External stresses such as work pressures, insufficient time for personal life, difficult living conditions, poor climate or frequent moves take their toll on our coping ability in conflict situations. This may be even truer of internal stress, such as fatigue, anxiety, unresolved internal conflicts, physical illness and hormonal imbalance.

When we recognize our stress and realize its effects, we can take it into consideration and be more caring of others. Whenever possible, don't attempt to manage major conflicts when you're overloaded with other stresses.

Think about Core Belief #4, then consider the following:

1. Mark on the scale, below, where your stress level is now.

    Low Stress <————————————————————————> High Stress

2. What, if anything, can you do about your stress level?

3. How does stress affect your communities?

4. When intense external and internal stress affect your ability to manage conflict, how do you normally act?

5. What could you change in relation to stress and conflict to help your relationships?

---

4 Stress Busters for Missionaries gives proven, biblical skills to help lower your stress. Learn more in the Appendix.

Core Belief #5

Spiritual resources are vital for managing conflicts.

Think about Core Belief #5, then answer these questions:

1. Could an outsider who observes your relationships tell that you are a servant of Christ? Why or why not?

2. How are you at using these resources?

   a. Studying the Word to discover which spiritual resources you can apply in your relationships, in handling conflicts.

   b. Consciously claiming Christ's power for your relationships.

   c. Praying with and for others regularly.

   d. Making use of godly counsel in times of need.

   e. Seeking to apply biblical principles in your relationships. One way is to make a daily commitment to clothe yourself with compassion, kindness, humility, gentleness and patience, as commanded by God in Colossians 3:12 (NIV).

3. Which of the above resources do you need to apply better? How will you do that?

4. Do you really believe (and act on it) that spiritual resources will help you manage conflict? If not, is this something that would be helpful for you by changing your core belief?

Core Belief #6

Healthy relationships involve mutually building each other up.

Those who seek only to be at peace with others often run into trouble because the scriptural pattern for relationships includes building up one another.

Think about Core Belief #6. Then answer these questions.

1. What do these verses tell you about this core belief?

    Romans 14:19 (HCSB): "We must pursue what promotes peace and what builds up one another." When we strive for both of these goals we are more apt to help rather than react negatively to weaknesses in each other.

    Romans 15:1–2 (NIV): "We who are strong ought to bear with the failings of the weak, and not to please ourselves. Each of us should please our neighbors for their good, to build them up." When we bear with each other's failings and try to please each other, we have a foundation upon which to build up one another in the Lord.

    Ephesians 4:29 (NIV): "Do not let any unwholesome talk come out of your mouths, but only what is helpful for building others up according to their needs, that it may benefit those who listen." Let's make this a goal in our relationships.

2. Are you living as if you believe this core belief? Why or why not?

3. What might you need to change to begin applying this in your communities?

Now that we've looked at core beliefs and how they affect our relationships, let's look at a few ground rules that give any conflict greater success.

Ground Rules

Here are some "Dos" and "Don'ts" for being effective in conflict management. Discuss these ground rules with those in your communities. Decide which you want to try to follow when you have conflicts. Applying these biblical principles will increase your chances of finding a solution you're both happy with.

Things to Do for Effective Conflict Management

1. **Take your problem to the Lord first.** Ask Him to show *you* what you might be doing to aggravate the problem. If the problem is a onetime event rather than a continuing source of irritation, you may be able to resolve it alone with the Lord by forgiving and bearing with the other person. What do these verses tell you?

   Proverbs 19:11 (AMP): "Good sense makes a man restrain his anger, and it is his glory to overlook a transgression or an offense."

   Proverbs 27:5–6 (NLT): "An open rebuke is better than hidden love! Wounds from a sincere friend are better than many kisses from an enemy."

   Colossians 3:13 (NIV): "Bear with each other and forgive one another if any of you has a grievance against someone. Forgive as the Lord forgave you."

   However, don't run away from ongoing problems by over spiritualizing or by denying that your feelings are valid and need handling. Ask God for wisdom to know whether to overlook the offense or to confront the issue.

2. **Deal with conflicts as soon as possible.** Ephesians 4:26 (NKJV) says, "'Be angry, and do not sin': do not let the sun go down on your wrath." This provides a healthy principle for handling anger: attempt to resolve the conflict the same day it comes up.

   Feelings are like cement—they begin to harden quickly. You can't always handle a situation immediately, but agree together to bring things up the same day when possible.

   Jumping into an issue the instant it comes up, without thinking through and praying first, is dangerous too. Wisdom is needed. Take time to pray and to allow the Holy Spirit to speak to you. Though it's important to resolve differences quickly, never do so while upset or angry. Quell your anger before any attempts at resolution.

3. **Keep to the present.** Don't bring up past problems. Talk about what is happening now. When you say, "You always ..." or "You never ...," you automatically bring up the past. Proverbs 17:9 (NLT) says, "Love prospers when a fault is forgiven, but dwelling on it separates close friends."

4. **Concentrate on one issue.** Proverbs 20:3 (NIV) says, "It is to one's honor to avoid strife, but every fool is quick to quarrel." To avoid unnecessary strife, make sure you know exactly what is bothering you, and keep to that one issue. Don't bring up unrelated problems. When more than one issue is thrown in, discussion can break down into a hopeless quarrel.

    When another issue legitimately comes up as part of the first, stop and decide whether it must be resolved before handling the original issue.

5. **Use "I statements."** In expressing feelings, state clearly how you feel rather than attacking or blaming. For example say, "I feel hurt and disappointed when I'm criticized in front of others," rather than, "Why do you always have to criticize me in front of others?"

    Look at Paul's "I statements" in 2 Corinthians 2:1–4 (ESV): "I made up my mind not to make another painful visit to you. For if I cause you pain, who is there to make me glad but the one whom I have pained? And I wrote as I did, so that when I came I might not suffer pain from those who should have made me rejoice, for I felt sure of all of you, that my joy would be the joy of you all. For I wrote to you out of much affliction and anguish of heart and with many tears, not to cause you pain but to let you know the abundant love that I have for you."

    Beware of hiding an attack inside an "I statement," such as, "I feel that you're a hateful, inconsiderate jerk!" Instead consider saying something like, "I felt hurt when you said I'm selfish and uncaring."

    What does Proverbs 16:21, 23–24 (NKJV) tell you? "The wise in heart will be called prudent, and sweetness of the lips increases learning. The heart of the wise teaches his mouth, and adds learning to his lips. Pleasant words are like a honeycomb, sweetness to the soul and health to the bones."

6. **Establish and observe "belt lines."** Each of you should make clear what kinds of remarks "hit below the belt." These are comments designed only to hurt. If you catch yourself hitting below the belt, stop and ask forgiveness immediately.

Be careful your words don't crush the other person's spirit. Proverbs 18:14 (NIV) says, "The human spirit can endure in sickness, but a crushed spirit who can bear?"

Accept responsibility for what you say when you're angry. If the other person begins to hit below the belt, mention it immediately. Don't let it pass by because it can be too damaging to ignore.

7. **Express feelings appropriately.** Let each other know how you feel during a disagreement. If you are angry, frustrated or disappointed, talk about your feelings, using "I statements." But avoid just venting your anger. Don't use a sledge hammer to swat a fly!

   If you're given to exploding, try getting alone and venting it to the Lord first. This can be a good way to let off steam, and He is big enough to take your temper without being hurt.

   What do these verses say to you?

   Proverbs 29:11 (ESV): "A fool gives full vent to his spirit, but a wise man quietly holds it back."

   Proverbs 15:18 (NLT): "A hot-tempered person starts fights; a cool-tempered person stops them."

   Proverbs 29:22 (ESV): "A man of wrath stirs up strife, and one given to anger causes much transgression."

Things Not to Do in Conflict

1. **Don't attack each other's character.** Proverbs 11:12 (NIV) says, "Whoever derides their neighbor has no sense, but the one who has understanding holds their tongue."

   Talk about behavior rather than personality. "It's really hard to keep the house clean when papers and clothes are left lying around" is less inflammatory than "Why do I have to live with the town slob?" Attacks easily degenerate into character assassination.

2. **Don't mind read.** Don't try to analyze each other's motives and thoughts. It's easy to think we understand the *why* behind others' behavior, but we don't have the right to tell them what their motives are, and then condemn them for those motives. Proverbs 20:5 (CJB) says, "The heart's real intentions are like deep water; but a person with discernment draws them out."

3. **Don't make predictions.** Ecclesiastes 10:14 (ESV) says, "A fool multiplies words, though no man knows what is to be, and who can tell him what will be after him?" Be careful about predicting how someone will react in actions, thoughts or feelings. The fact that he reacted in a certain way before doesn't mean he will do so this time. Give him an opportunity to respond in the way you would like him to respond.

4. **Don't counterattack.** When someone brings up a problem, be willing to talk about it without reference to his failures and weaknesses. Attacking him guarantees that even a small conflict will escalate into full-blown war. If he is hurt by something you're doing, allow him to share his feelings and then work together to find a solution. This means setting aside your desire to avoid blame by laying it on him.

What do these verses tell you?

1 Peter 2:22–23 (ESV): "He committed no sin, neither was deceit found in his mouth. When he was reviled, he did not revile in return; when he suffered, he did not threaten, but continued entrusting himself to him who judges justly."

1 Peter 3:8–11 (NIV): "Be like-minded, be sympathetic, love one another, be compassionate and humble. Do not repay evil with evil or insult with insult. On the contrary, repay evil with blessing, because to this you were called so that you may inherit a blessing. For, 'Whoever would love life and see good days must keep their tongue from evil and their lips from deceitful speech. They must turn from evil and do good; they must seek peace and pursue it.'"

5. **Don't try to be the winner.** This may seem odd, but any attempt to win at the expense of the other destroys your unity in Christ. A desire to win usually means getting the best of the other person—getting *your way at his expense.* When one of you loses, *both lose* because the conflict is not truly resolved. Mutually satisfactory solutions *are* possible with God's enabling, if both of you can give up the idea of winning.

6. **Don't seek revenge.** Do not allow yourself to say or even think, "I'll pay you back for what you did." Revenge has no place in Christian relationships. Yet it's easy to give in to it. If you feel vengeful, admit it to the Lord and decide to give it up to Him.

You may be tempted to get back at the person—and it may feel justified. However, revenge will severely damage any attempts at reconciliation.

What do these verses tell you?

Proverbs 24:29 (ESV): "Do not say, 'I will do to him as he has done to me; I will pay the man back for what he has done.'"

Romans 12:17–21 (NIV) applies to all relationships! It says, "Do not repay anyone evil for evil. Be careful to do what is right in the eyes of everyone. If it is possible, as far as it depends on you, live at peace with everyone. Do not take revenge, my dear friends, but leave room for God's wrath, for it is written: 'It is mine to avenge; I will repay,' says the Lord. On the contrary: 'If your enemy is hungry, feed him; if he is thirsty, give him something to drink. In doing this, you will heap burning coals on his head.' Do not be overcome by evil, but overcome evil with good."

7. **Don't dump your problem on other people.** Secretly telling a friend not only betrays the person you are having a conflict with, it may make you more resentful. Proverbs 20:19 (NIV) says, "A gossip betrays a confidence."

On the other hand, it may help to talk to a pastor, counselor or close friend who will be honest with you and give ideas for resolution. Watch your motives! Are you looking for genuine help or for sympathy?

Questions for Personal or Group Study

Consider the following alone or with a group:

1. Review this Key.

    a. What stands out for you?

    b. Write down any areas in which you need to improve. What will you do to grow in each area?

2. What can you learn about managing conflict from the following Scriptures? What do they tell us about how to react when there are disagreements?

Matthew 18:15–17 (ESV): "If your brother sins against you, go and tell him his fault, between you and him alone. If he listens to you, you have gained your brother. But if he does not listen, take one or two others along with you, that every charge may be established by the evidence of two or three witnesses. If he refuses to listen to them, tell it to the church. And if he refuses to listen even to the church, let him be to you as a Gentile and a tax collector."

1 Corinthians 13:1–7 (ESV): "If I speak in the tongues of men and of angels, but have not love, I am a noisy gong or a clanging cymbal. And if I have prophetic powers, and understand all mysteries and all knowledge, and if I have all faith, so as to remove mountains, but have not love, I am nothing. If I give away all I have, and if I deliver up my body to be burned, but have not love, I gain nothing. Love is patient and kind; love does not envy or boast; it is not arrogant or rude. It does not insist on its own way; it is not irritable or resentful; it does not rejoice at wrongdoing, but rejoices with the truth. Love bears all things, believes all things, hopes all things, endures all things."

Ephesians 4:31–32 (NLT): "Get rid of all bitterness, rage, anger, harsh words, and slander, as well as all types of evil behavior. Instead, be kind to each other, tenderhearted, forgiving one another, just as God through Christ has forgiven you."

3. Go over the core beliefs again.

   a. Discuss with your spouse or a good friend whether or not you agree on each of them, and how strongly you hold these. To what degree are they demonstrated in your family? What about in your other relationships?

   b. Talk about Core Belief #4, and how stress affects your relationships as a couple, as a friend, with your children or with your coworkers.

What can you begin to do differently? For example, you can *talk* out your stress, rather than *acting* out your stress.

4.   Look over the "Ground Rules" again.

   a.   Consider which ones you follow in your closest relationships.

   b.   Which ground rules do you violate at times? What about with your spouse, children and/or other close relationships? You may want to ask their forgiveness.

5.   Write out any commitments for change you want to make before the Lord.

A Verse to Meditate On and Memorize

Choose a verse from this chapter. If you are not sure which to choose, try this one:

Psalm 133:1 (NIV): "How good and pleasant it is when God's people live together in unity!"

Snapshots

Go to the section titled "Snapshots" to record points you want to remember and/or do.

Chapter 3

Fight a Winning Battle

A hot-tempered person stirs up conflict, but the one who is patient calms a quarrel.
Proverbs 15:18 NIV

In this chapter, you'll discover:
- Eight practical steps you can take to successfully manage differences
- Thirteen nonverbal ways to defuse resistance
- Sixteen verbal methods to neutralize resistance
- Six questions for personal or group study

Can you relate? I hope not! I had a "friend" who, no matter what the conflict, had to win.[1] She never stopped talking long enough to listen to anything I had to say. No matter what I tried to say, I was shot down. She acted like saying more words would prove she was right. It didn't. It just proved she could talk a lot. Needless to say, we were never able to resolve any issues between us, so the relationship was not able to go deeper.

How do you handle conflict? People have a wide variety of ways to handle conflict; some are more effective than others. Some use words, either unkind or kind. Others use their fists or body language. Some use intonation or volume, yelling or speaking softly. Others openly express anger, while others hold it inside and let it simmer.

Others seek revenge. I ordered an ice cream cone in a drive-through one summer. The employee told me it would be one hundred and thirty-eight pennies. I joked with him and said, "I don't think I have that many." He then told me how he handled a conflict with his former wife. He paid her last alimony payment in pennies! He dumped three hundred thousand pennies on her front porch!

---

1 Names and details in stories are changed to protect the innocent—and not-so-innocent.

In this chapter we look at a specific strategy to help you deal with conflicts, even if the other person doesn't use the same skills. However, if both use this strategy, it is much more likely to result in restored and even transformed relationships.

It's important to note that nothing always works. You may use the best skills, yet nothing seems to help lower the other person's anger. Those are times when all you can do is give it to the Lord, asking for His wisdom and grace.

A Suggested Strategy for Managing Conflicts

No one procedure is ideal for everyone, but this method gives helpful guidelines for managing conflicts well. You may find it cumbersome and artificial at first, but it will be worth the effort. After you try it, you can modify it to fit your particular relationship. The following description implies that both of you are following the ground rules and strategy. However, even if you are the only one following them, you greatly increase the probability of success.

1. **Take the issue to God.** When you're bothered about something another person is doing, tell God how you feel and confess any desire for retribution. Don't hesitate to freely express your feelings to Him, using "I statements," preferably aloud. Or write God a letter. This process usually helps calm your feelings and may help sort out the issues.

    Consider these questions before the Lord:
    - Is this problem a onetime event which I can forgive and forget, without bringing it up?
    - Is this a real issue or a trivial one that hides a deeper grievance?
    - Is it primarily my problem and not the other person's? If so, am I willing to give it up?
    - Am I willing to be honest and caring?
    - Am I ready to present a specific request for change?

    Before going to the person, ask God for a spirit of gentleness according to Galatians 6:1 (NLT): "Dear brothers and sisters, if another believer is overcome by some sin, you who are godly should gently and humbly help that person back onto the right path. And be careful not to fall into the same temptation yourself."

    Make a commitment to "clothe yourself" with compassion, kindness, humility, gentleness and patience, according to Colossians 3:12. Ask Him to prepare your heart.

What do these verses tell you?

Proverbs 14:17, 29 (NKJV): "A quick-tempered man acts foolishly, and a man of wicked intentions is hated. ... He who is slow to wrath has great understanding, but he who is impulsive exalts folly."

Proverbs 15:18 (NIV): "A hot-tempered person stirs up conflict, but the one who is patient calms a quarrel."

In Chapter 4, you'll gain more ideas in the *"Conflict Management Checklist."*

2. **Bring up the issue.** Open the issue with a statement like, "I've got a concern I need to talk over. When is a good time?" Timing is crucial. Ecclesiastes 3:7–8 (AMP) says, "A time to rend and a time to sew, a time to keep silence and a time to speak, a time to love and a time to hate, a time for war and a time for peace." It may or may not be wise to describe what the problem is at this point. If he asks what you want to talk about, you can briefly tell him, so you don't keep him in suspense. Agree on a time when you will meet together.

3. **Explain the conflict.**
   - Share what the problem is and how you feel about it.
   - Keep your statements short and simple.
   - State exactly what the person does (or doesn't do), and how it affects you, without attacking him. Focus on the observable behavior(s), not on inferences, attitudes or assumptions.
   - The other person should listen carefully and give feedback at frequent intervals.
   - He should put into his own words his understanding of what is wrong and how you feel about it.
   - He should not defend himself or counterattack.

As the other person listens and shows understanding, the intensity of your feelings will probably lessen, especially if he can accept them with a loving attitude. This in no way implies he agrees—only that he acknowledges your feelings as real without judging you.

What do these verses say to you?

James 1:19 (NLT): "Understand this, my dear brothers and sisters: You must all be quick to listen, slow to speak, and slow to get angry."

Proverbs 15:1 (AMP): "A soft answer turns away wrath, but grievous words stir up anger."

Proverbs 15:28 (NIV): "The heart of the righteous weighs its answers, but the mouth of the wicked gushes evil."

Proverbs 17:27 (ESV): "Whoever restrains his words has knowledge, and he who has a cool spirit is a man of understanding."

Proverbs 18:2 (NKJV): "A fool has no delight in understanding, but in expressing his own heart."

Proverbs 24:26 (NLT): "An honest answer is like a kiss of friendship."

"Crusty" feelings such as anger, fury, exasperation and frustration often surface in a conflict. But these repel the other person, and make it very difficult to respond with empathy. Crusty feelings make a poor basis for conflict resolution.

Underneath those harsh emotions almost always lay "tender" feelings such as hurt, disappointment, sadness, loneliness and feeling unimportant. If you can listen in a caring way and patiently draw out these tender feelings from each other, you'll draw closer and be much more motivated to resolve your conflicts.

4. **Propose a tentative solution.** Next, state what you would like to be done to correct the problem, realizing this is an initial attempt to find a mutually satisfactory solution. Also say what it would mean to you and how it might benefit both of you. Or you may ask him for a possible solution. Proverbs 16:21 says that *pleasant words* are persuasive (NLT).

    The other person should give frequent feedback to demonstrate understanding. It isn't enough to say, "I understand." He should be able to accurately describe in *his own words* what you want and what it would mean to both of you. When you're sure he understands, you may go to the next step.

5. **The other person responds to you.** This is his opportunity to tell how he feels about the issue and your proposal for solving it. Statements

should be short and simple, so you can put them into your own words and thus demonstrate you understand. He needs the same acceptance and understanding you received earlier.

The other person has three alternatives at this point:

- He may agree with your request.
- He may disagree completely.
- He may suggest an alternative solution—a totally new proposal or a modification of yours.

He might be willing to go along with you if you concede to counter requests. Application of Philippians 2:3–4 by *both* of you can make this process not only possible, but a joyful experience. It says, "Don't be selfish; don't try to impress others. Be humble, thinking of others as better than yourselves. Don't look out only for your own interests, but take an interest in others, too" (NLT).

If you come to an agreement, try to negotiate a contract for change. This is a verbal or written agreement stating what each of you will try to do so that hopefully the problem will be resolved. If you can agree, go on to Step 7. But if you can't agree on a solution in a short time, go to Step 6.

6. **Take an intermission, if needed.** If a solution isn't reached quickly, let the issue rest for a day or two. It's usually much easier to discover a solution when you allow time for God to reveal creative alternatives and to bring healing for hurt feelings. Decide on a time for coming back to the issue, and commit your feelings to God for the time being. Pray He will give each of you wisdom and willingness to find a solution which will be a win/win situation.

When you come back together, determine which step you need to begin with. It will probably be either Step 4 or 5.

7. **Ask for and grant forgiveness to each other.** Unresolved anger or resentment will destroy a relationship. Before a conflict can be totally resolved, these feelings must be dealt with. In this step, both of you need to ask for forgiveness. This doesn't necessarily imply you were wrong or you intentionally hurt each other. It means you acknowledge one another's hurt, and you both want to be free from any resentment that may have come up.

Make sure your request for forgiveness doesn't come across as a *demand* that the other person forgive you! It should be a humble acknowledgment of your desire for it rather, than a demand.

Then decide to forgive each other in the power of Christ, and talk about it. This act of love allows God to neutralize your feelings. You may find you can work through this step better alone with the Lord rather than together. Remember, forgiveness is a process and usually takes some time. As you work through the process, demonstrate your forgiveness by your actions.

Apply these verses to your relationship:

1 Corinthians 13:5 (NIV): "[Love] does not dishonor others, it is not self-seeking, it is not easily angered, it keeps no record of wrongs."

Colossians 3:13 (NIV): "Bear with each other and forgive one another if any of you has a grievance against someone. Forgive as the Lord forgave you."

8. **Afterward, review the conflict alone and together.** Take time to rethink the conflict. Summarize what you both understood and agreed on. Express any differences and what you learned from this experience. You might ask how you can pray for each other.

   See "Conflict Management Checklist" in Chapter 4 for ideas.

Conclusion

Even if the other person is unaware of these concepts or is unwilling to follow them, you can apply the ground rules and attempt to follow the steps to some degree.

This approach *may* seem cumbersome! However, this very fact can help you to concentrate on the process of resolving your disagreements. It slows down the process to enable you to work at it step by step, and it helps reduce inappropriate expression of feelings. Yes, it does take effort to master. But if you do, you will dramatically improve your ability to manage your conflicts effectively. Try it and see.

Some Ways of Defusing Resistance in Conflict

Any time you are in a conflict situation, including confronting and responding to a verbal attack, people can become very resistant. Here are a few ways that can help defuse the resistance.

- Look through the verbal and nonverbal ways to defuse resistance.
- Check the items you need to use more effectively.

Defuse Resistance—Nonverbally

- ❏ Appear calm.
- ❏ Face the person.
- ❏ Keep an open posture.
- ❏ Keep a distance that is safe for him; don't sit or stand too close.
- ❏ Give appropriate eye contact, maintaining it without staring.
- ❏ Speak quietly and gently.
- ❏ Speak slowly.
- ❏ Listen without interrupting.
- ❏ Persevere; do not give up.
- ❏ Do not raise your voice.
- ❏ Do not act agitated (even if you feel agitated).
- ❏ Do not act angry (even if you feel angry).
- ❏ Give the benefit of the doubt as to motives.

Defuse Resistance—Verbally

- ❏ Agree with whatever you can.
- ❏ State in your own words what the person said.
- ❏ Ask for clarification if needed.
- ❏ Affirm the relationship.
- ❏ Appeal to the relationship, stating how important it is to you.
- ❏ Try to keep to the issue at hand.
- ❏ If there are several issues, ask which issue he wants to start with.
- ❏ Express gratitude for anything he does right.
- ❏ Ignore attacks on your character.
- ❏ Ask, "What would you like from me?"
- ❏ Ask, "Can I share with you how I am impacted by this now?"
- ❏ Ask to get together later if he does not control his anger.
- ❏ Suggest that a neutral party join you.
- ❏ Try to resolve the problem.
- ❏ Do not respond defensively.
- ❏ Do not counterattack when accused.

Look at the boxes you checked.

1. Which issues do you think could most help your communities?

2. Pick two or three concerns from the list you will begin working on immediately. Specifically, what will you do to improve in these areas?

3. How can improving the items you marked improve relationships in your communities?

Questions for Personal or Group Study

Consider the following alone or with a group:

1. Review this Key.

   a. What stands out for you?

   b. Write down any areas in which you need to improve. What will you do to grow in each area?

2. Proverbs 13–17 gives many principles for managing conflict. Read the chapters, personalize any principles that speak to you and write them in your own words. Here are two examples:

   Proverbs 13:3 (MSG): "Careful words make for a careful life; careless talk may ruin everything."

Proverbs 14:17 (MSG): "The hotheaded do things they'll later regret; the coldhearted get the cold shoulder."

3. Consider the steps of "A Suggested Strategy for Managing Conflicts."

   a. Which of these steps do you usually follow when you have a conflict in your home, at work, or in other contexts?

   b. Which steps do you want to begin incorporating?

4. Look at "Some Ways of Defusing Resistance in Conflict." Share with someone you trust which ones you are working to improve.

5. Ask your spouse, older children, friends and/or coworkers what they would like you to do differently when you have a disagreement with them.

6. Write a commitment to grow in any areas where God is convicting you; then share your commitment with someone who will help you be accountable.

A Verse to Meditate On and Memorize

Choose a verse from this chapter. If you are not sure which to choose, try this one:

> Proverbs 15:18 (NIV): "A hot-tempered person stirs up conflict, but the one who is patient calms a quarrel."

Snapshots

Go to the section titled "Snapshots" to record points you want to remember and/or do.

Chapter 4

How Am I at Managing Conflicts?

Repay no one evil for evil, but give thought to do what is honorable in the sight of all.
Romans 12:17 ESV

Now that you've studied the principles for managing conflict, you have an opportunity to assess how you are currently doing. These assessments are not tests to receive a grade, but rather an opportunity for you to determine any areas where you may need to work.

In this chapter, you will do two different assessments. Then you will look at a "Conflict Management Checklist" you can use before, during and after a conflict to help you evaluate how you are doing.

How Am I at Managing My Conflicts?

In this, and in many of the other assessments, you will have a chance to evaluate how you are doing with your family as well as with others in your life. The difference in the results can be eye-opening. It is often natural for people not to treat their family as well as others. As you go through this assessment, be totally honest. That's the only way you can grow in needed areas.

Consider how you are doing at managing your conflicts using this scale to indicate your responses.

1 = Hardly ever, 2 = Occasionally, 3 = Sometimes,
4 = Often, 5 = Nearly always

Family Others

_____ _____ 1. I prayerfully consider the best time and place to bring up a conflict.

_____ _____ 2. When a conflict arises, I am consciously aware that our relationship is almost always more important than the issue.

_____ _____ 3. If possible, I take time to pray and think about it before jumping into a conflict.

_____ _____ 4. I avoid clamming up and refusing to talk when I'm in a conflict situation.

_____ _____ 5. When I'm in a conflict with someone, I resist trying so hard to get my way that I endanger our relationship.

_____ _____ 6. I am able to forgive, even when the offender hasn't asked for forgiveness or expressed a desire for it.

_____ _____ 7. When the timing is appropriate, I ask for forgiveness if the person has been hurt or offended by me, whether I believe I was wrong or not.

_____ _____ 8. I use "I statements" rather than "you statements" whenever possible.

_____ _____ 9. I avoid saying "you always ..." and "you never ..." when in conflict.

_____ _____ 10. I listen carefully to the other person's point of view and try to put what he is saying into my own words before responding with my point of view.

_____ _____ 11. I keep to the one issue at hand rather than bringing up several issues at a time.

_____ _____ 12. I am very careful not to say things that are deliberately meant to hurt.

_____ _____ 13. I resist trying to read the other person's mind and making prophecies about how they will react.

_____ _____ 14. I refrain from attacking the person's character and focus on behavior as much as possible.

_____ _____ 15. I am honest with my feelings and express them in ways that are appropriate to the person and the situation.

Look over your responses to "How Am I at Managing My Conflicts?"

1. Congratulate yourself! Did you score a 4 or a 5 in any of the statements above? If so, you are doing great!

2. Needs Improvement. Prayerfully consider each of your 1s and 2s.

   a. Write an action plan to improve each area of concern.

   b. Choose one or two to begin working on right now.

3. Once you have improved the 1s and 2s, work on the 3s.

4. Talk with someone who will hold you accountable.

   a. With whom will you talk?

   b. When will you call?

Hypothetical Scenarios

Read through the following real-life situations. Then answer the questions following each. These can help you determine how you currently handle conflict and any areas where you might improve.

Missions Trip. You are on a team at your mission with several other people planning to take volunteers and ministry partners on a mission trip. One of the people, Sue, feels very strongly that the team has to go back to Nicaragua, where you served last time. She says you need to follow up with those you served. You believe it would be beneficial to go to a different location so you can learn to adapt to different cultures, people and ministries. The others on the team don't have strong feelings about the decision. You are at an impasse. What can you do so the team isn't destroyed but you are not just giving up?

1. How would you naturally respond to this situation?

2. What have you learned from this Key to help you manage this conflict more effectively?

3. Look back over "Ground Rules" to overcome conflict in Chapter 2. Which would be most difficult for you to apply in this situation?

4. In what specific areas do you think you will struggle most to deal with this conflict?

5. Which ways to defuse resistance might help most in this situation?

6. How can you prepare yourself to handle a situation like this?

7. If you apply the guidelines in this Key, what do you think the outcome might be?

Two Leaders in Conflict. You are a supervisor in your mission. Your boss is trying to make the work environment friendlier. He asks you and Peter to figure out how to do it so members will have greater contentment. Up until now, people have been required to work 8:00 to 5:00, with no exceptions. You think people should be able to pick their own hours as long as they get a full day of work done. Peter feels strongly that will create chaos in the office. Supervisors won't be able to keep tabs on what their members are doing. You believe more work will be accomplished because people will work when their minds are the most alert. You both have very strong opinions on this topic. How can you resolve it in a God-honoring way?

1. How would you naturally respond to this situation?

2. What have you learned from this Key to help you manage this conflict more effectively?

3. Look back over "Ground Rules" to overcome conflict in Chapter 2. Which would be most difficult for you to apply in this situation?

4. In what specific areas do you think you will struggle most to deal with this conflict?

5. How can you prepare yourself to handle a situation like this?

6. If you apply the guidelines in "A Suggested Strategy for Managing Conflicts" (in Chapter 3), what do you think the outcome might be?

7. Which ways to defuse resistance might help most in this situation?

Conflict Management Checklist

Use this checklist before and after conflicts you know are coming up.

Pre-Conflict Check: When You Can Anticipate a Conflict Situation

1. Preparing My Heart

   Have I honestly considered *why* I'm bringing up this conflict? _____

   Have I acknowledged my negative feelings and begun working on resolving them? _____

   Have I surrendered any wrong attitudes and motivations to God? _____

   Have I asked Him to prepare the other person's heart and help him to be willing to find a resolution we can live with? _____

   Is there anything else I need to talk over with God first? _____

2. Preparing What to Say (How to Begin)

   Do I have the *essential issue* clearly in mind and am I able to clearly state it? _____

   Am I prepared to honestly and lovingly share my *feelings* about this matter? _____

   Do I have a clear understanding of what I would like to see happen? _____

3. Preparing for the Context

   Have I decided on the best *time* to bring up the issue? _____

   Have I decided on the best *location*? _____

Post-Conflict Check and Comments

1. Did I clearly and specifically present the issue in dialogue? _____

2. Were we able to keep the conversation to one present issue? _____

3. Did I appropriately control and express my feelings? _____

4. Did I avoid attacks, mind reading, prophesying and counterattacks? _____

5. Did I effectively present ideas for possible solutions? _____

6. Did I listen well without interrupting, yet giving feedback and adequate opportunity to express feelings, perceptions and solutions? _____

7. Did we find a mutually acceptable solution, resulting in a minimum of unresolved feelings and misunderstanding? _____

8. If we couldn't agree, did I do everything possible to preserve our relationship? _____

9. Have we set up a time for ongoing dialogue, if needed? _____

Questions for Personal or Group Study

Consider the following alone or with a group:

1. Review this Key.

    a. What stands out for you?

    b. Write down any areas in which you need to improve. What will you do to grow in each area?

2. What can you learn about managing conflict from the following Scriptures?

    Deuteronomy 19:15 (ESV): "A single witness shall not suffice against a person for any crime or for any wrong in connection with any offense that he has committed. Only on the evidence of two witnesses or of three witnesses shall a charge be established."

    Luke 6:27–28 (NLT): "To you who are willing to listen, I say, love your enemies! Do good to those who hate you. Bless those who curse you. Pray for those who hurt you."

Romans 12:17–21 (ESV): "Repay no one evil for evil, but give thought to do what is honorable in the sight of all. If possible, so far as it depends on you, live peaceably with all. Beloved, never avenge yourselves, but leave it to the wrath of God, for it is written, 'Vengeance is mine, I will repay, says the Lord.' To the contrary, 'if your enemy is hungry, feed him; if he is thirsty, give him something to drink; for by so doing you will heap burning coals on his head.' Do not be overcome by evil, but overcome evil with good."

1 Corinthians 4:13 (ESV): "When slandered, we entreat. We have become, and are still, like the scum of the world, the refuse of all things."

3.   Consider what God says about someone who stirs up conflict.

Proverbs 6:16–19 (NIV): "There are six things the Lord hates, seven that are detestable to him: haughty eyes, a lying tongue, hands that shed innocent blood, a heart that devises wicked schemes, feet that are quick to rush into evil, a false witness who pours out lies and *a person who stirs up conflict in the community.*" (emphasis added)

Proverbs 6:12–14 (NIV): "A troublemaker and a villain, who goes about with a corrupt mouth, who winks maliciously with his eye, signals with his feet and motions with his fingers, who plots evil with deceit in his heart—*he always stirs up conflict.*" (emphasis added)

4.   When you have a disagreement with someone in your community, ask him what he would like you to do differently in the next conflict situation.

5. If you are working in a team, as well as in your family, review this Key
    with them.

    a. Discuss each core belief to see whether you all hold them to be true.
        If not, you may need to determine what your team's or family's core
        beliefs are in each area.

    b. Discuss the "Ground Rules" and try to agree to follow them when
        there is a conflict.

6. Based on what you learned in this Key so far, write two or three things
    you will do differently the next time a conflict comes up.

A Verse to Meditate On and Memorize

Choose a verse from this chapter. If you are not sure which to choose, try
this one:

> Romans 12:17 (ESV): "Repay no one evil for evil, but give thought to
> do what is honorable in the sight of all."

Snapshots

Go to the section titled "Snapshots" to record points you want to remember
and/or do.

Chapter 5

How Can Conflict Improve My Relationships?

If possible, so far as it depends on you, live peaceably with all.
Romans 12:18 ESV

In this chapter you will have an opportunity to practice the skills you've learned. Here are activities you'll do.

1. Observe two skill demonstrations and write your observations:[1]

   a. How *Not* to Manage Conflict

   b. How to Manage Conflict Well

2. Practice managing a conflict with a partner. Find your partner before you watch the demonstration so you can discuss what you observe.

3. Review what you learned from role-playing the skill.

Before You Start

If you don't already have one or more people with whom you are studying this book, I urge you to find someone. In order to get the most out of this study, you need to practice the skills

Review the Ground Rules to Manage Conflict

First, take time to review the ground rules for managing conflict. If you need to, you can go back to Chapter 2 to understand each one more fully.

---

1 You can get access to the demonstrations at http://rddemos.rrbooks.org.

What to do:

1. Take your problem to the Lord first.
2. Deal with conflicts as soon as possible.
3. Keep to the present.
4. Concentrate on one issue.
5. Use "I statements."
6. Establish and observe "belt lines."
7. Express feelings appropriately.

What to avoid doing:

1. attacking each other's character
2. mind reading
3. making predictions
4. counterattacks
5. trying to win
6. seeking revenge
7. dumping your problem on others

Demonstrations of Skills

As you watch the video demonstrations, keep in mind:

1. You'll see show how to apply the skills to a conflict.
2. You can apply what you see in the second demonstration in your own life.
3. You don't have to be a trained counselor to apply what you see.
4. Watch for the principles from this Key that are demonstrated, rather than looking at what you would do differently.
5. Avoid getting caught up in the issue.

Demonstration #1: How NOT to Manage Conflict

In this demonstration, the people *break* as many ground rules as possible. As you watch, write your observations on the chart below.

1. What ground rules were broken?

2. What was said or done to break the ground rules?

Verbally	Nonverbally

Demonstration #2: How to Manage Conflict Well

In this demonstration, the demonstrators *follow* as many ground rules as possible. As you watch, write your observations on the chart below.

1. What ground rules were observed?

2. What was said or done to follow the ground rules?

Verbally	Nonverbally

After the demonstration, talk with your role-play partner:

1. What did you observe?

2. What other things could have been said or done?

3. What differences did you see between the two demonstrations?

Practice Managing a Conflict

Take time to practice managing a conflict. Practicing has great benefits, including the following:

- Applying this skill in a safe environment reinforces your responses when faced with conflict in real life.
- You will gain confidence in a real confrontation, because you were successful in the practice.
- Your relationships will improve as you become more adept at dealing with conflict as it arises.
- The opportunity to receive feedback improves your conflict resolution skills.

Do the following:

1. Choose an issue to use as you practice. This could be:

   a. A situation you or someone you know experienced before.

   b. A situation you are facing now.

   c. One of the hypothetical scenarios from Chapter 4.

2. As you practice, do the following:

   a. Focus on applying steps from "A Suggested Strategy for Managing Conflicts."
      - o Explain the conflict.
      - o The other person listens carefully and gives feedback at frequent intervals.
      - o Propose a tentative solution.
      - o The other person responds to you.

   b. Concentrate on using "I statements," listening and giving feedback.

3. Afterward, talk about what you learned with your practice partner:

   a. What would you do differently in a real situation?

   b. What did you learn from that experience?

Questions for Personal or Group Study

Consider the following, alone or with a group:

1. Review this Key.

    a. What stands out for you?

    b. Write down any areas in which you need to improve. What will you do to grow in each area?

2. What can you learn about managing conflict from this passage?

    1 Corinthians 6:1–8 (NIV): "If any of you has a dispute with another, do you dare to take it before the ungodly for judgment instead of before the Lord's people? Or do you not know that the Lord's people will judge the world? And if you are to judge the world, are you not competent to judge trivial cases? Do you not know that we will judge angels? How much more the things of this life! Therefore, if you have disputes about such matters, do you ask for a ruling from those whose way of life is scorned in the church? I say this to shame you. Is it possible that there is nobody among you wise enough to judge a dispute between believers? But instead, one brother takes another to court—and this in front of unbelievers! The very fact that you have lawsuits among you means you have been completely defeated already. Why not rather be wronged? Why not rather be cheated? Instead, you yourselves cheat and do wrong, and you do this to your brothers and sisters."

3. Get together with a family member, friend or coworker and study this Key together and practice the steps using a real or hypothetical conflict situation. If you have had trouble handling conflict with the person in the past, start with a hypothetical scenario so you can focus on applying the skills rather than getting caught up in the issues.

4. In your mission:

   a. Go over this Key with the people on your team.

   b. Discuss the core beliefs to see if you all hold them. If not, what might need to change so you aren't in conflict over them?

   c. Try to agree together to follow the ground rules when there is a conflict. You might want to come up with a code word to remind you to apply them to the current situation.

   d. Watch the demonstrations together and practice the skill.

   e. Talk about how you can hold each other accountable for using the skills in this Key.

5. You could use the above points with your family, friendships or small groups as well.

A Verse to Meditate On and Memorize

Choose a verse from this chapter. If you are not sure which to choose, try this one:

Romans 12:18 (ESV): "If possible, so far as it depends on you, live peaceably with all."

Snapshots

Go to the section titled "Snapshots" to record points you want to remember and/or do.

Strategy for Success

This is your opportunity to look at a conflict situation in your life that you may not have resolved well or haven't yet resolved. You can evaluate how you did at managing the conflict and what you may need to do differently in the future.

1. Write an account of a past or current conflict situation.

2. What have you learned from this Key that could help you resolve the issue?

Key #2: To Err Is Human—to Confront Is Divine

Most people shy away from dealing with difficult issues. Is confrontation scary to you? It doesn't have to be. Often people think it is more difficult than it is. This section outlines a simple process that can leave your relationships strengthened rather than undermined.

Chapter 6

A Call to Engage

If your brother sins against you, go and tell him his fault,
between you and him alone.
If he listens to you, you have gained your brother.
Matthew 18:15 ESV

Before I began teaching a workshop for missionaries on interpersonal skills, I greeted one of the participants, whom I barely knew. She noticed I had lipstick on my teeth and quietly told me, so no one else even heard. I was so grateful, because I didn't realize it. I would have been embarrassed to have taught the session and later discovered it.

You may wonder why I start with such a simple example. Are you thinking, "That's not confronting." Most of us have a wrong view of confronting. In reality, biblical confrontation is often simply pointing out a blind spot in someone else. Dictionary.com defines it as a "meeting of persons face to face; an open conflict of opposing ideas, forces, etc.; a bringing together of ideas, themes, etc., for comparison." Most people only focus on the negative side of confrontation, rather than on its positives.

Are you comfortable with confronting? Is it something you look forward to? For many of us, confronting is one of *the* most difficult parts of relating to others, yet it is essential to godly relationships. God's Word has numerous verses and examples of confrontations.

Dr. Dorothy Gish studied over four hundred Christian workers from various organizations and countries. Of sixty stressors, "confronting others when necessary" was the most frequently mentioned. More than 50 percent said they experienced "considerable" to "great" stress over confronting!

Reasons People Avoid Confrontation:

- **People's reactions:** Have you confronted anyone who then exploded in anger? A person's response can make you hesitant to try again.
- **Fear:** Are you afraid you will look bad? Do you fear rejection or not being understood?
- **Discomfort:** Is confronting someone too uncomfortable? Not knowing how the other person will respond can generate negative thoughts and feelings that prevent you from confronting.
- **Other Reasons:** What other reasons keep you from confronting?

Positive Outcomes of Confronting

Do you think of confronting as negative? Look at some possible positive results of confronting.

- It rejuvenates each person's knowledge, understanding and respect for each other.
- It reconnects you with the other person.
- It resolves misunderstandings and promotes harmony.
- It reveals "blind spots." These are areas where you cannot see yourself clearly because you lack information and/or skills. Confronting someone's blind spot helps the other person grow.
- It opens up the lines of communication and invites interaction.

Is Confrontation Optional?

Consider this: to fail to confront when it is our responsibility may be sin. We tend to view confronting others as optional in the Christian life. But we need to see it as seriously as God does. What do these verses say to you?

Proverbs 10:10 (NIV): "Whoever winks maliciously causes grief, and a chattering fool comes to ruin."

Proverbs 24:11 (ESV): "Rescue those who are being taken away to death; hold back those who are stumbling to the slaughter."

Ephesians 4:25–27 (NLT): "Stop telling lies. Let us tell our neighbors the truth, for we are all parts of the same body. And 'don't sin by letting anger control you.' Don't let the sun go down while you are still angry, for anger gives a foothold to the devil."

James 5:19–20 (AMP): "[My] brethren, if anyone among you strays from the Truth and falls into error and another [person] brings him back [to God], let the [latter] one be sure that whoever turns a sinner from his evil course will save [that one's] soul from death and will cover a multitude of sins [procure the pardon of the many sins committed by the convert]."

Proverbs 24–25. Read these chapters, writing down all you learn from them about confrontation.

Confrontation is one of the difficult parts of relating to others, yet it is essential for good relationships in our communities.

Consider

Think back to the last time you needed to confront:
- Did you confront the person? If so, how did it go? If not, did the problem get worse because you didn't confront?

- How did you feel before and during the confrontation?

- What was the person's response?

- What could you have done differently?

Now think about the following:

- What do you do when you're upset with someone—whether it's an team member, ministry partner, pastor, someone you are serving, a friend or family member? Note: You may react differently to different people.

- How do you diffuse conflict in your relationships before they blow up into time-consuming crises?

- What do people in your community do when they are upset with someone else? (This could be people in your family, church, mission and other communities.)

- Are you happy with the answers to the above questions? If not, study this Key well and have your community study it together and practice the skills. Consider having a training organization such as Relationship Resources come in to help you grow in these skills.

What if you were told after you gave the greatest presentation of your life that few, if any, like it—that the principles were confusing, the examples simplistic and the delivery boring. While hard to accept, wouldn't you prefer for someone to tell you rather than to say nothing at all?

Confrontation can be as simple as someone telling you that you have jam on your face or resolving a jam in which you find yourself with another person.

Core Beliefs about Confronting

Remember: your core beliefs determine how you live your life. Consider each of the core beliefs below to determine whether they accurately reveal how you live. If they don't, ask God to show you what you may need to change.

Summary: a core belief is a firmly held conviction that consistently motivates my behavior.

Belief + Consistent Action = Core Belief

Core Belief #1

Good confrontation is dialogue, not monologue.

Think about Core Belief #1 and answer these questions:

1. What does this mean to you in your communities?

2. When you confront, do you normally use dialogue or monologue? Explain.

3. If you normally use monologue when confronting, what has been the resulting outcome? If the outcome was more negative than positive, what could you change to make the outcome more positive?

4. In relation to Core Belief #1, what could you change to help your relationships?

Core Belief #2

Being an effective _____ *requires effective confronting.*

Write down each role in your life that fits Core Belief #2. For example, "Being an effective parent requires effective confronting."

_____ parent _____	_____
_____	_____
_____	_____
_____	_____
_____	_____
_____	_____
_____	_____
_____	_____
_____	_____
_____	_____
_____	_____
_____	_____
_____	_____
_____	_____

Can you think of any role in your life where you don't need to be a skillful confronter?

Core Belief #3

It takes _____ to confront well.

What qualities do you need to confront well? For example, you may say, "It takes courage and respect to confront well." List every quality you need in order to confront well.

courage	
respect	

Many people think confronting is harsh and negative. However, if done wisely and respectfully, it is one of the best ways to help others—as well as to grow yourself.

Training every person in your community in confrontation skills is vital to your success. People will confront others when they get angry, but *how* they confront can dramatically affect your whole group. If they confront in anger, they may cause others to leave your group or be pushed away from ever wanting to join. Either way, you and your group lose.

Questions for Personal or Group Study

Consider the following alone or with a group:

1. Review this Key.

    a. What principles and ideas about confronting stand out for you?

    b. Write down any areas in which you need to improve. What will you do to grow in each area?

2. Examine these proverbs and write any insights you gain about confronting.

    Proverbs 15:1 (NIV): "A gentle answer turns away wrath, but a harsh word stirs up anger."

    Proverbs 15:4 (ESV): "A gentle tongue is a tree of life, but perverseness in it breaks the spirit."

    Proverbs 16:24 (ESV): "Gracious words are like a honeycomb, sweetness to the soul and health to the body."

Proverbs 25:15 (NIV): "Through patience a ruler can be persuaded, and a gentle tongue can break a bone."

Proverbs 27:5–6 (NIV): "Better is open rebuke than hidden love. Wounds from a friend can be trusted, but an enemy multiplies kisses."

3. How stressful is confronting for you? Ask the Lord to help you to see it as He sees it.

4. What are reasons you avoid confronting?

5. Review your answers to the questions under, "Consider."

   a. What did you learn about your thinking process when having to confront?

   b. How does confronting impact your feelings? Your body? Your sleep? Eating patterns? Relationships with others?

6. Share your answers to the core beliefs with someone close to you. When you share, especially the items in Core Beliefs 2 and 3, you'll recognize other areas you may have missed:

    a. Being an effective _____ requires effective confronting.

    b. It takes _____ to confront well.

A Verse to Meditate On and Memorize

Choose a verse from this chapter. If you are not sure which to choose, try this one:

Matthew 18:15 (ESV): "If your brother sins against you, go and tell him his fault, between you and him alone. If he listens to you, you have gained your brother."

Snapshots

Go to the section titled "Snapshots" to record points you want to remember and/or do.

Chapter 7

Rules of Engagement

A gentle answer turns away wrath, but a harsh word stirs up anger.
Proverbs 15:1 NIV

My friend Suzi,[1] another missionary, said some very mean things to me and about me. After prayerfully considering what to say, I told her how much I appreciated her friendship. Then I confronted her about how much her words hurt me. Her immediate response was to get very angry and begin blaming me. She said I deserved everything that was said. Then she started telling me everything she didn't like about me. I listened, not knowing what I could say to stop her barrage.

Once she began to calm down, I was able to tell her how her words hurt me. I listened when she told me why she said what she did. When I shared my feelings, she apologized. I asked her to come to me in the future if she was upset with me. She began to understand how her words could damage. That conversation drew us much closer together than we had ever been. If I hadn't been willing to risk confronting her, I probably would have drifted away from the relationship, and she may never have known why.

Sometimes when we confront someone, they respond positively, but other times, like with Suzi, they respond very negatively. What we do then determines what the outcome might be, although no matter what we do, we can't force the other person to react well. All we can do is follow some guidelines and pray.

In this chapter we will look at specific guidelines you can use when confronting anyone. Most of these guidelines come directly from the Bible.

---

1 Her name and details have been changed.

Guidelines for Confronting

You may think avoiding or ignoring the issue will make it go away, but it rarely will. Ask yourself, "What kind of member of my community (name the community) am I, if I am unwilling to confront to forge the way toward more effective communication and understanding?"

In this section, we'll look at how to prepare for a confrontation, then the actual event and finally a review of how it went.

Prepare for the Confrontation

1. **Define your goal.** Winning, wounding, insulting, punishing, hurting or manipulating someone to get what you want are inappropriate goals. What positive outcome, understanding or resolution are you aiming for? Be clear about your purpose. Always confront to strengthen, restore or heal the relationship.

2. **Before confronting, spend sufficient time in prayer and consider all the issues.** Some people tend to jump into confrontation too quickly without thinking through all the concerns and ramifications. On the other hand, do not spend so much time thinking about the situation that you never get around to confronting.

    Here are suggestions for your prayer time:
    *   Confess any destructive attitudes, feelings or actions to God.
    *   Ask Him to give you a loving, caring attitude toward the person.
    *   Ask Him to guide you and give you the right words.
    *   Pray the other person will be open to receive what you have to say.

3. **Learn how to confront effectively in the specific culture where you find yourself.** To a great degree, confrontational skills are culturally defined. American society is a conglomeration of many cultures. You will deal with many backgrounds during your life and relationships. Discover what is considered appropriate confrontation for each specific culture you work with and what you should avoid doing when confronting them.

4. **Evaluate the situation.** What issue do you need to confront? Observe the truth so you can address the issue in the most positive and objective way. Make a list:
    *   What is fact?
    *   What is feeling?

- What is conjecture? You normally don't want to share this with the person, especially if it is negative.

For example, I may be angry because my tenant was late on his payment again. I believe he is just a deadbeat, so I want to kick him out of my home. However, he has been there for over a year and for the most of that time his payments have been on time.

- **What is fact?** He is late on his payment for a second time, but he is usually on time.
- **What is feeling?** I'm frustrated and angry because I didn't have his payment, so I couldn't pay the mortgage.
- **What is conjecture?** He is a deadbeat.

5. **Determine how your being offended or hurt has resulted in a breach in your relationship.** Unresolved hurts are barriers to communication. To remove communication obstacles, let go of the offense. Why allow the bite of the offense to deepen into a cancerous wound? If done well, willingness to confront

- removes distance;
- restores mutual trust;
- honors the relationship and the other person.

If the person has offended or hurt you or is doing things that bother you, work on bearing with and forgiving him before confronting. These eliminate the desire to avoid the person and they open the doors of communication once more.

What do these verses say to you about this?

Romans 15:1 (NIV): "We who are strong ought to bear with the failings of the weak and not to please ourselves."

Colossians 3:12–14 (NIV): "As God's chosen people, holy and dearly loved, clothe yourselves with compassion, kindness, humility, gentleness and patience. Bear with each other and forgive one another if any of you has a grievance against someone. Forgive as the Lord forgave you. And over all these virtues put on love, which binds them all together in perfect unity."

6. **Avoid letting your feelings influence how you confront.** Do you like or dislike the person? Does how you feel affect your decision to confront?

- If he is your friend or you don't want to hurt him, do not dodge confrontation.

- If you are biased against him, avoid using confrontation to punish or retaliate.

These verses give teaching on both situations. What can you learn from them?

Proverbs 26:28 (NLT): "A lying tongue hates its victims, and flattering words cause ruin."

Proverbs 27:5 (AMP): "Open rebuke is better than love that is hidden."

Proverbs 29:5 (NKJV): "A man who flatters his neighbor spreads a net for his feet."

Romans 12:17–21 (ESV): "Repay no one evil for evil, but give thought to do what is honorable in the sight of all. If possible, so far as it depends on you, live peaceably with all. Beloved, never avenge yourselves, but leave it to the wrath of God, for it is written, 'Vengeance is mine, I will repay, says the Lord.' To the contrary, 'if your enemy is hungry, feed him; if he is thirsty, give him something to drink; for by so doing you will heap burning coals on his head.' Do not be overcome by evil, but overcome evil with good."

7. **Seek to resolve the issue with the person rather than gossiping about him.** Venting your thoughts or feelings with others or involving others pollutes the problem. Problems compound when you vent.

What do these verses tell you?

Proverbs 25:9–10 (NIV): "If you take your neighbor to court, do not betray another's confidence, or the one who hears it may shame you and the charge against you will stand."

Proverbs 25:23 (ESV): "The north wind brings forth rain, and a backbiting tongue, angry looks."

1 Peter 2:1 (NLT): "Get rid of all evil behavior. Be done with all deceit, hypocrisy, jealousy, and all unkind speech."

8. **Set up a convenient time to meet with the person.** Determine a time and place where neither of you will have distractions. Timing is essential. However, do not avoid the confrontation because there is not a perfect time.

What do these verses say about timing?

Proverbs 29:20 (NIV): "Do you see someone who speaks in haste? There is more hope for a fool than for them."

Ecclesiastes 3:7 (NLT): "[There is] a time to tear and a time to mend. A time to be quiet and a time to speak."

9. **Review "Some Ways of Defusing Resistance in Conflict" from Chapter 3** to be prepared for any resistance.

Confronting: The Encounter

The key to a successful outcome depends on your manner of confronting. If you have an amicable approach, the person is less likely to be defensive or resistant. Remember, these principles work in your personal life as well as in your professional life. Here are a few guidelines for confronting:

1. **Speak the truth.** If there is any doubt as to the truth, use tentative statements or questions. For example, listen attentively and then say:
   - "It sounds like you are saying _____. Is that what you meant?"
   - "Can you explain to me what you just said?"

   What do these verses say to you?

   Proverbs 12:17 (NIV): "An honest witness tells the truth, but a false witness tells lies."

   Ephesians 4:15 (ESV): "Speaking the truth in love, we are to grow up in every way into him who is the head, into Christ."

2. **Confront clearly and concisely**. State what is fact, what is feeling, and what is conjecture. Clearly focus on the following:

   a. **What you observe.** What did you see or experience that you need to confront? Be as specific as possible.

   b. **How you or others are affected.** To break down defensiveness and resistance, talk about how you are affected by the behavior.

   c. **What you want to see happen.** Explore options to resolve the issue. Be willing to agree to disagree, negotiate or come to an agreement.

3. **Be aware of your nonverbal communication.**[2] Realize that you may be confronting others nonverbally through silence, facial expression, body language and tone of voice. For example, you may say positive words, but your nonverbal communication may reveal to the person that you dislike them. Negative nonverbal confrontation is

   • difficult for the other person to receive;
   • rarely effective;
   • often harmful to the relationship.

4. **Confrontation is most effective when you consistently affirm the person.** In every relationship, get in the habit of regularly telling people what you appreciate about them.

   Proverbs 27:6 (ESV) says, "Faithful are the wounds of a friend; profuse are the kisses of an enemy." The word "friend" implies this kind of relationship. In this situation, confronting usually helps the relationship become stronger.

   However, if you haven't affirmed the person consistently, use the "sandwich approach":

   • Acknowledge the person's positive intentions or behavior.
   • Confront the issue or behavior.
   • Positively reinforce the person.

   Sandwiching the "meat" of the issue between a positive statement and a compliment preserves or strengthens the relationship.

   Always end with reaffirming your relationship. Let the other person know that you value him and your relationship.

5. **If you are angry, do not use the confrontation to "dump garbage" on the person.** Garbage-dumping includes the following:

---

2 You can get a free 50-page eBook on nonverbal communication at rrfree.info.

- Bringing up past issues, either from this relationship or problems with other people
- Putting the person down
- Calling names

Although some expression of anger may be appropriate, deal with the cutting edge of your anger before the confrontation. Otherwise, it may degenerate into nothing more than an argument.

What do these verses say about this?

Proverbs 12:18 (NIV): "The words of the reckless pierce like swords, but the tongue of the wise brings healing."

Proverbs 29:11 (NLT): "Fools vent their anger, but the wise quietly hold it back."

James 1:19–20 (AMP): "Understand [this], my beloved brethren. Let every man be quick to hear [a ready listener], slow to speak, slow to take offense and to get angry. For man's anger does not promote the righteousness God [wishes and requires]."

6. **Confront behavior rather than character or personality.** Most judging of others involves the latter two areas. Attacking or criticizing character or personality is hurtful and unproductive. To provide a platform to address behavior problems, focus on the specific conduct you see and how it affects you. When addressing specific behavior, say, "When you (state their behavior), I feel …"

Galatians 2:11–14 (NIV) gives an example. What does this passage say to you?

"When Cephas [Peter] came to Antioch, I opposed him to his face, because he stood condemned. For before certain men came from James, he used to eat with the Gentiles. But when they arrived, he began to draw back and separate himself from the Gentiles because he was afraid of those who belonged to the circumcision group. The other Jews joined him in his hypocrisy, so that by their hypocrisy even Barnabas was led astray. When I saw that they were not acting in line with the truth of the gospel, I said to Cephas in front of them all, 'You are a Jew, yet you live like a Gentile and not like a Jew. How is it, then, that you force Gentiles to follow Jewish customs?'"

7. **When your feelings are involved, use** "I messages" rather than "you messages." When you use an "I message," you take responsibility for your feelings rather than blaming the other person for how you feel.
   - "I message": "I am angry."
   - "You message": "You make me mad."

Look at Paul's "I messages" when he confronted the Corinthian Christians. What can you learn from them? For example:

2 Corinthians 2:4 (NKJV): "Out of much affliction and anguish of heart I wrote to you, with many tears, not that you should be grieved, but that you might know the love which I have so abundantly for you."

2 Corinthians 12:20–21 (ESV): "I fear that perhaps when I come I may find you not as I wish, and that you may find me not as you wish—that perhaps there may be quarreling, jealousy, anger, hostility, slander, gossip, conceit, and disorder. I fear that when I come again my God may humble me before you, and I may have to mourn over many of those who sinned earlier and have not repented of the impurity, sexual immorality, and sensuality that they have practiced."

To find other examples, read through the book of 2 Corinthians.

8. Be open to receiving confrontation as well as to giving it. When it is appropriate, ask the person you are confronting for feedback. You can also invite him to confront you when he sees negative actions or traits in your life. Only do this with people you trust to confront you lovingly.

What do these verses say to you about this?

Proverbs 15:10 (NKJV): "Harsh discipline is for him who forsakes the way, and he who hates correction will die."

Proverbs 15:12 (NLT): "Mockers hate to be corrected, so they stay away from the wise."

9. **Effective confrontation is a dialogue between two people rather than monologue.** It's important to listen to the other person. Just as you want to be understood, the other person also wants to be heard. So don't just talk, listen. The next Key deals with this topic in greater detail.

10. **Your manner of confronting is crucial.** Here are a few specific guidelines with Scriptures on the topic:

   a. **Confront gently.** Avoid harshness or anger.

   Proverbs 15:4 (NLT): "Gentle words are a tree of life; a deceitful tongue crushes the spirit."

   Galatians 6:1 (ESV): "Brothers, if anyone is caught in any transgression, you who are spiritual should restore him in a spirit of gentleness. Keep watch on yourself, lest you too be tempted."

   2 Timothy 2:25 (NKJV): "In humility [correct] those who are in opposition, if God perhaps will grant them repentance, so that they may know the truth."

   b. **Confront patiently.** It is not always easy to hear constructive insights.

   Proverbs 25:15 (NIV): "Through patience a ruler can be persuaded, and a gentle tongue can break a bone."

   1 Thessalonians 5:14 (ESV): "We urge you, brothers, admonish the idle, encourage the fainthearted, help the weak, be patient with them all."

   c. **Use pleasant speech whenever possible.**

   Proverbs 16:21 (AMP): "The wise in heart are called prudent, understanding, and knowing, and winsome speech increases learning [in both speaker and listener]."

   Proverbs 16:23 (NIV): "The hearts of the wise make their mouths prudent, and their lips promote instruction."

   d. **Avoid arguing or quarreling.**

   Proverbs 17:14 (NIV): "Starting a quarrel is like breaching a dam; so drop the matter before a dispute breaks out."

   Proverbs 18:19 (ESV): "A brother offended is more unyielding than a strong city, and quarreling is like the bars of a castle."

   2 Timothy 2:25 (NLT): "Gently instruct those who oppose the truth. Perhaps God will change those people's hearts, and they will learn the truth."

e. **Avoid rash words.** Confront for healing rather than for punishing or hurting. Also avoid using generalities, such as "you always," or "you never."

Proverbs 12:18 (NKJV): "There is one who speaks like the piercings of a sword, but the tongue of the wise promotes health."

Ephesians 4:31–32 (NIV): "Get rid of all bitterness, rage and anger, brawling and slander, along with every form of malice. Be kind and compassionate to one another, forgiving each other, just as in Christ God forgave you."

After the Confrontation

1. **Judge the effectiveness of the confrontation by whether you see long-term change in behavior and/or attitudes.** The person's immediate reaction is not the best indicator of the effectiveness of the confrontation. It is common for a person to respond poorly, but then change his mind later. Others may seem to respond well at first, but do not truly change.

2. **If confrontation does not go well, don't automatically blame yourself.** Look at how effectively you confronted, but also realize that the ultimate responsibility for change belongs to the other person. Several of Jesus' confrontations "failed" humanly speaking.

Look at these passages and write what you learn from them:

Matthew 19:16–22 when Jesus talked with the rich man.

Matthew 21:33–46 where Jesus confronted the Pharisees. As a result, they looked for a way to arrest him.

Summary

Confrontation is essential for your relationships; however, it is not easy for most people. Failing to confront small problems often causes them to intensify.

Review this chapter several times. Practice confrontation with a friend or someone in one of your communities. As you do so, you will gain greater proficiency at using this skill and your relationships will improve.

Questions for Personal or Group Study

Consider the following alone or with a group:

1. Review this Key.

   a. What stands out for you?

   b. What is the most difficult part for you? Why? What might you need to change?

2. Study "Guidelines for Confronting."

   a. Look up each Scripture. Pick a few to memorize or meditate on.

   b. Consider how you are doing at applying them to your relationships.

   c. Discuss with someone close to you which guidelines are the most difficult for you.

3. The next time a situation comes up where you believe you need to confront, look over the "Guidelines for Confronting" and work at applying them. Afterward, look them over again and consider how well you did and what you may want to do differently the next time you must confront.

4. What can you learn from these verses that will help you when confronting?

Ephesians 4:15 (NIV): "Speaking the truth in love, we will grow to become in every respect the mature body of him who is the head, that is, Christ."

1 Thessalonians 5:14 (NKJV): "We exhort you, brethren, warn those who are unruly, comfort the fainthearted, uphold the weak, be patient with all."

2 Timothy 2:24–25 (RSV): "The Lord's servant must not be quarrelsome but kindly to every one, an apt teacher, forbearing, correcting his opponents with gentleness. God may perhaps grant that they will repent and come to know the truth."

Job 33:6–7 (NIV): "I am the same as you in God's sight; I too am a piece of clay. No fear of me should alarm you, nor should my hand be heavy on you."

Proverbs 19:11 (ESV): "Good sense makes one slow to anger, and it is his glory to overlook an offense."

Proverbs 28:23 (NKJV): "He who rebukes a man will find more favor afterward than he who flatters with the tongue."

Matthew 18:15–17 (NLT): "If another believer sins against you, go privately and point out the offense. If the other person listens and confesses it, you have won that person back. But if you are unsuccessful, take one or two others with you and go back again, so that everything you say may be confirmed by two or three witnesses. If the person still refuses to listen, take your case to the church. Then if he or she won't accept the church's decision, treat that person as a pagan or a corrupt tax collector."

5. Write down any areas in which you need to improve in your confrontation skills. What will you do to grow in each area?

A Verse to Meditate On and Memorize

Choose a verse from this chapter. If you are not sure which to choose, try this one:

Proverbs 15:1 (NIV): "A gentle answer turns away wrath, but a harsh word stirs up anger."

Snapshots

Go to the section titled "Snapshots" to record points you want to remember and/or do.

Chapter 8

How Am I at Confronting?

Brothers, if anyone is caught in any transgression,
you who are spiritual should restore him in a spirit of gentleness.
Keep watch on yourself, lest you too be tempted.

Galatians 6:1 ESV

Self-evaluation is extremely important for our personal growth. It gives us the opportunity to determine how we are doing in our relationships. This chapter has two types of assessments:

1. In the first, you evaluate how you are currently doing at confronting—both with people in your family or anyone else you are close to and other people. You may be surprised what you learn about the differences in how you confront family versus other people.

2. In the second assessment, you'll read two hypothetical stories and answer questions to determine how you would normally react to those situations and how you could improve.

How Am I at Confronting When Necessary?

Consider how you are doing at confronting, and use this scale to indicate your responses.

1 = Hardly ever, 2 = Occasionally, 3 = Sometimes,
4 = Often, 5 = Nearly always

Family Others

____ ____ 1. Before confronting I ask God for wisdom, gentleness and love in the way I confront.

_____ _____ 2. When I have a problem with someone, I prayerfully consider whether it is best to joyfully seek to accept the person and the situation or to confront.

_____ _____ 3. Before confronting I consider what the issue is, how it affects me and/or others, and what I would like to happen.

_____ _____ 4. I take into consideration the other person's culture before confronting.

_____ _____ 5. Before confronting, I try to quiet my anger and fear by expressing them to God.

_____ _____ 6. I don't let my fears keep me from confronting when I know I should.

_____ _____ 7. When I'm hurt or offended by someone, I don't avoid them.

_____ _____ 8. I confront in a loving and gentle way even when I'm angry.

_____ _____ 9. When someone is hurting or offending me by their behavior, I resist acting as though everything is fine.

_____ _____ 10. If I know there is a problem between another person and me, I take the initiative rather than waiting for him to come to me.

_____ _____ 11. I practice the core belief that "good confronting is dialogue" by listening to and seriously considering the other person's point of view when confronting.

_____ _____ 12. I readily admit any part I have in the problem.

_____ _____ 13. I go directly to the person with whom I'm having the conflict rather than gossiping about him to others.

_____ _____ 14. I try to choose the best time and place to confront.

_____ _____ 15. I avoid confronting when others are around unless they need to be in on it.

Look over your responses to "How Am I at Confronting When Necessary?"

1. **Congratulate yourself!** Did you score a 4 or a 5 in any of the statements above? If so, you are doing great!

2. **Needs Improvement.** Prayerfully consider each of your 1s and 2s.

    a. Write an action plan to improve each area of concern and consider what barriers cause you the most distress.

    b. Choose one or two to begin working on right now.

    c. Once you have improved the 1s and 2s, work on the 3s.

3. Talk with someone who will hold you accountable.

    a. With whom will you talk?

    b. When will you call?

Now, let's look at two fictional stories to see how you might react to them.

Hypothetical Scenarios

Read through these real-life situations. Then answer the questions following each.

Someone Is Gossiping about You. You love your mission and your team. You made a commitment to one another not to talk with anyone outside the group about what was shared when you are together. This helped you feel safe to share your struggles. However, recently you discovered that Sara, one of your friends in the group, told several people about your struggles. You found out because two of them came up to you and said, "I'm praying for you about your situation. Sara knew I would pray for you so she told me in confidence."

1. How would you usually respond in this situation?

2.   What have you learned from this Key that could help you respond better?

3.   Look back over "Guidelines for Confronting" in Chapter 7. What would you need to do to prepare to confront Sara?

4.   What are your objectives for this confrontation?

5.   In what areas would you most struggle in the confrontation?

6.   How do you think Sara might respond if you use the skills you learned in this Key?

7.   If you don't use this Key's guidelines, what might the outcome be?

8.   How can you prepare yourself to handle a situation like this? Remember, situations like this are not unusual.

An Member of Your Mission Is Not Working Full Hours. You are on staff at your mission, supervising five people. You notice James has been coming in late and leaving early most days without an explanation. He snapped at someone else who noticed how little he is working yet still getting paid his full salary. You know you need to talk to him, but aren't sure how or when to do it.

1. How would you usually respond in this situation?

2. What have you learned from this Key that could help you respond better?

3. Look back over "Guidelines for Confronting" in Chapter 7. What would you need to do to prepare to confront James?

4. What are your objectives for this confrontation?

5. In what areas would you most struggle in the confrontation?

6. How do you think James might respond if you use the skills you learned in this Key?

7. If you failed to use this Key's guidelines, what might the outcome be?

8. How can you prepare yourself to handle a situation like this?

Times When Confrontation Is Ineffective

There are some times when confrontation may not be effective and may even have a negative outcome. Some people thrive on conflict, dishonesty and betrayal. To confront them would be futile. Some people may harm you or others if you try to confront them.

Here is an example from a friend, "We were scammed and lost over $1300 to a guy whose business is scamming. I used these principles, only to be shunned. His attitude was 'This is really a small amount and you shouldn't be concerned about it. You got caught in my web and paid the price. End of story.'" For someone who knowingly is a liar and a thief, confronting is useless. He possesses no conscience and justifies all his actions based on selfish ends.

When You Can't Confront Face-to-Face

Confronting in person is normally the best way to do it so you can see the person's nonverbal communication as well as them seeing yours. However, there are times we must confront someone even though we can't be with them in person. This can also be very effective if done well. Here are some possible ways you can do this:

1. *Writing a paper letter.* This can be a powerful way to confront, even if the person is close enough to talk face-to-face. It forces you to clearly think through what you want to say and it gives you a chance to let the material sit a while before sending. This period of "sitting" often proves very helpful since it allows you to check the content for any angry feelings or innuendos that might convey negativity.

2. *Sending an e-mail.* This can be very dangerous unless you include the reflective waiting time. Angry feelings need time to dissipate and be replaced with reasoned judgment. I've confronted this way and it's worked well, but I let the e-mail sit for a day or two before I send it. Often I will let someone else read it to make sure it comes across well.

3. *Making a phone call.* In this case, you have some of the nonverbal communication, including intonation, inflection and volume. However you are missing body language. I urge you to use the "sandwich technique." Begin with an upbeat, nonthreatening personal story, such as "I just saw a wonderful movie you would enjoy," and explain why. If possible, tie in a theme from the story to the reason for your call. Be concise about your concern, avoiding rabbit trails. Offer time for the

other person to respond. Give one or two suggestions for resolution. Try to end on an upbeat note by summarizing what you agreed upon and, if appropriate, connect it once again your initial story.

Questions for Personal or Group Study

Consider the following alone or with a group:

1. Review this Key.

    a. What stands out for you?

    b. Write down any areas in which you need to improve. What will you do to grow in each area?

2. Reflect on Paul's "I statements" as he confronted the Galatians. What was Paul communicating through these statements?

    Galatians 1:6 (NIV): "I am astonished that you are so quickly deserting the one who called you to live in the grace of Christ and are turning to a different gospel."

    Galatians 4:11 (NIV): "I fear for you, that somehow I have wasted my efforts on you."

    Galatians 4:20 (ESV): "I wish I could be present with you now and change my tone, for I am perplexed about you."

    Galatians 5:10 (NLT): "I am trusting the Lord to keep you from believing false teachings. God will judge that person, whoever he is, who has been confusing you."

3. Look over your responses to "How Am I at Confronting When Necessary?" Especially consider anywhere you rated yourself a score of three or less. Decide what you want to begin working on, and what you will begin doing differently. Share your commitment with someone who will hold you accountable.

4. Discuss with your spouse or close friend:

   a. "What would you like me to do differently when I confront you?"

   b. "One thing I would like to do differently when I confront you is …"

   c. "Is there anyone in our lives whom we've needed to confront but haven't? What will we do about it?"

5. Read 2 Samuel 12:1–14 to see how Nathan confronted David. What do you think about the method he used? How could you use that same technique?

6. Review the hypothetical scenarios. Which one would you struggle with the most? Why? What might help you?

A Verse to Meditate On and Memorize

Choose a verse from this chapter. If you are not sure which to choose, try this one:

> Galatians 6:1 (ESV): "Brothers, if anyone is caught in any transgression, you who are spiritual should restore him in a spirit of gentleness. Keep watch on yourself, lest you too be tempted."

Snapshots

Go to the section titled "Snapshots" to record points you want to remember and/or do.

Chapter 9

How Can I Confront More Effectively?

Faithful are the wounds of a friend; profuse are the kisses of an enemy.
Proverbs 27:6 ESV

In this chapter, you have an opportunity to practice the skills you've learned. Here are activities you'll do.

1. Review the "Guidelines for Confronting" from Chapter 7.

2. Watch two skill demonstrations:

   a. The first demonstration[1] shows a person being confronted and receiving it well.

   b. In the second demonstration, the person will receive it poorly.

3. Practice confronting with a partner in a safe environment. You'll practice this twice, once after each demonstration.

4. Review what you learned from role-playing the skill.

Preparation

Watch the demonstrations with a friend, coworker or family member who also wants to grow in his skills. Then take turns practicing confronting with that person.

The demonstrations show how to apply the skill of effective confrontation. Remember the following:

1. The people in the video may not handle the situation like you would.

2. They don't show anything that you can't apply. You don't have to be a trained counselor to confront others.

---

1 You can get access to the demonstrations at http://rddemos.rrbooks.org.

3. Avoid getting caught up in the issue they are dealing with. Rather watch for the principles you learned from this Key.

Review of Guidelines for Confronting

As you watch the demonstrations and when you practice confronting, keep this list with you to remind you of what to do.

1. Speak the truth.

2. Confront clearly and concisely.

3. Be aware of your nonverbal communication.

4. Confrontation is most effective when you consistently affirm the person.

5. If you are angry, do not use the confrontation to "dump garbage" on the person.

6. Confront behavior rather than character or personality.

7. When your feelings are involved, use "I messages" rather than "you messages."

8. Be open to receive confrontation as well as to give it.

9. Effective confrontation is a dialogue between two people, not a monologue.

10. Your manner of confronting is crucial.

   a. Confront gently.

   b. Confront patiently.

   c. Use pleasant words.

   d. Avoid arguing or fighting.

   e. Avoid rash generalities, such as "you always" or "you never."

Demonstration #1: Confront Effectively—When the Confrontee² Receives It Well

This demonstration may seem unreal because people don't often receive confrontation well. But watch for the principles you learned. As you watch the first demonstration, write the following:

1. Verbal statements and behaviors you observe the confronter saying

2. Nonverbal actions you observe the confronter doing or not doing

Verbally	Nonverbally

After the demonstration, discuss with your partner:

1. What did the confronter *say* that was helpful in his confrontation?

2. What did he *do* that was helpful?

3. What would you have done differently?

---

2 The person being confronted.

Practice #1: Confront Effectively—When the Confrontee Receives It Well

Choose a Situation to Rehearse

1. Use the issue you saw demonstrated in the video.

2. Use a real issue you have experienced.

3. Choose an issue you are facing that you need to confront.

4. Or use one of these:

   a. Your coworker jokes about your idiosyncrasies.

   b. Your teammate talks about you behind your back.

   c. A member of your mission is loud and obnoxious in meetings.

   d. Your family member is treating you with disrespect.

What to Do

1. Decide which person will be the confrontee (the person being confronted).

2. The confrontee is to receive the confrontation well. He should not be defensive.

3. Follow the "Guidelines for Confronting."

4. After you practice, trade roles.

5. After you both have practiced, discuss with your role-play partner:

   a. What did you learn from this practice?

   b. What will you do differently in real life?

Demonstration #2: Confront Effectively—When the Confrontee Is Defensive

In this demonstration, the confrontee is defensive and resistant. The confronter will demonstrate how to overcome the resistance. Realize that in real life this would probably take much longer. For the sake of time, it is shortened. As you watch the second demonstration, write the following:

1. Verbal things you observe the confronter saying

2. Nonverbal actions you observe the confronter doing or not doing

Verbally	Nonverbally

After the demonstration, talk with your role-play partner about:

1. What did the confronter *say* that helped break down the person's resistance?

2. What did the confronter *do* that overcame the person's resistance?

3. What would you have done differently?

4. As a result of this practice, what could you apply in a real confrontation?

Practice #2: Confront Effectively—When the Confrontee Is Defensive

This time you have the opportunity to practice confronting someone who is defensive. Remember, practice is essential to develop any new skill. The less you enjoy confronting and the more you run from it the more you need to practice this skill in a safe environment until you become comfortable using it.

What to Do

1. Use the same situation you practiced in Practice #1.

2. This time, the confrontee should be defensive and counterattack. (If the confrontee is not defensive, then the person confronting will not have a good opportunity to practice this skill.)

3. The confronter is to try to break down resistance.

4. After a few minutes, the confrontee should lessen his resistance.

5. Then trade roles and practice again.

6. As you practice, be aware of what you're feeling, especially if you are the confrontee.

After You Practice

After you both have practiced, discuss with your role-play partner:

1. What did you learn from this practice?

2. What was most difficult for you?

3. Were there any surprises? If so, what?

4. What will you do differently in real life?

Questions for Personal or Group Study

Consider the following alone or with a group:

1. Review this Key.

    a. What stands out for you?

    b. Write down any areas in which you need to improve. What will you do to grow in each area?

2. Study this Key with your community—family, mission, team and so on.

    a. Discuss how well you are applying each guideline presented.

    b. What, if any, changes do you want to make as a group and/or individually?

    c. Discuss what you want to begin applying more diligently in your community.

    d. Make a commitment to lovingly confront each other when needed and to be open to receiving confrontation from each other.

3. For anyone in a leadership role, including parents, do the following:

    a. Consider: "What do I want to begin doing differently when I confront my children (or those under my leadership)?"

b. Ask them: "What would you like me to do differently when I talk to you about something you need to change?"

4. What can you learn about confronting through the following examples in Scripture? Study as many as you can. You might want to use these for your personal Bible study or in a small group.

Matthew 16:22–23 (NIV): "Peter took [Jesus] aside and began to rebuke him. 'Never, Lord!' he said. 'This shall never happen to you!' Jesus turned and said to Peter, 'Get behind me, Satan! You are a stumbling block to me; you do not have in mind the concerns of God, but merely human concerns.'"

Mark 10:21 (ESV): "Jesus, looking at [the rich man], loved him, and said to him, 'You lack one thing: go, sell all that you have and give to the poor, and you will have treasure in heaven; and come, follow me.'"

Luke 22:33–34 (NLT): "Peter said, 'Lord, I am ready to go to prison with you, and even to die with you.' But Jesus said, 'Peter, let me tell you something. Before the rooster crows tomorrow morning, you will deny three times that you even know me.'"

Luke 22:48 (AMP): "Jesus said to him, Judas! Would you betray and deliver up the Son of Man with a kiss?"

John 21:15–17 (ESV): "When they had finished breakfast, Jesus said to Simon Peter, 'Simon, son of John, do you love me more than these?' He said to him, 'Yes, Lord; you know that I love you.' He said to him, 'Feed my lambs.' He said to him a second time, 'Simon, son of John, do you love me?' He said to him, 'Yes, Lord; you know that I love you.' He said to him, 'Tend my sheep.' He said to him the third time, 'Simon, son of John, do you love me?' Peter was grieved because he said to him the third time, 'Do you love me?' and he said to him, 'Lord, you know everything; you know that I love you.' Jesus said to him, 'Feed my sheep.'" (Jesus asked Peter the same question three times.)

Galatians 2:11, 14 (NIV): "When Cephas [Peter] came to Antioch, I [Paul] opposed him to his face, because he stood condemned. ... I said to Cephas in front of them all, 'You are a Jew, yet you live like a Gentile and not like a Jew. How is it, then, that you force Gentiles to follow Jewish customs?'"

5. What was the most difficult part of practicing this skill? What was the easiest?

6. What areas do you need to work on to be able to confront more effectively? Pray with your practice partner for each other.

A Verse to Meditate On and Memorize

Choose a verse from this chapter. If you are not sure which to choose, try this one:

Proverbs 27:6 (ESV): "Faithful are the wounds of a friend; profuse are the kisses of an enemy."

Snapshots

Go to the section titled "Snapshots" to record points you want to remember and/or do.

Strategy for Success

This is your opportunity to look at a situation in your life you may not have resolved well or haven't yet resolved. You can evaluate how you did at confronting and what you may need to do differently in the future.

1. Write an account of a past or current situation.

2. What have you learned from this Key that could help you resolve the issue?

Key #3: Ticking Time Bombs

You can develop the skills to act when all you really want to do is react!

Many people put great emphasis on confronting well, but being able to *receive* it well is at least as important. God's Word probably has more to say about receiving confrontation than giving it. As we will see in this Key, Jesus is our model.

Have you ever had someone unexpectedly blow up at you? Some people are like time bombs—waiting to explode at a moment's notice. They can go off without warning. How can you react to a verbal attack so your relationship ends up stronger rather than being destroyed? This section reveals practical ways your reactions can dramatically affect the impact on your relationship when you feel attacked.

Chapter 10

Defusing a Ticking Time Bomb

Fools give full vent to their rage, but the wise bring calm in the end.
Proverbs 29:11 NIV

I'm writing this book in a remote cabin on two hundred acres, surrounded by national forest. Hummingbirds eagerly drink from the feeder I fill daily. Most of them get along and are willing to share. I've seen six birds drinking at once.

However, sometimes one bird attacks any others trying to feed. Even though he doesn't want to drink, he won't let the others drink either. His attacks with his beak are like what some people do with their words—confronting with anger. While I can't teach the birds how to get along, there are principles and skills you can learn so you can effectively handle verbal attacks against you.

Have you ever been ripped apart by someone's verbal rage? That kind of confrontation is unproductive. When a person is so angry that all he can do is scream, it's difficult to help him calm down enough so you can come to some kind of resolution.

Reflect

If you don't have a plan, you will react in your usual ways. Reflect on these questions:

1. How would you normally respond when someone verbally attacks you?

2. How might your typical response affect your family, friends, coworkers or community?

3. How could you respond better?

4. How might responding more effectively affect your relationships?

As you become proficient at responding well to verbal attacks, your relationships in your communities will improve. In this chapter, you will learn to

- defuse anger;
- resolve differences;
- maintain healthy relationships;
- achieve peace within yourself when you know you have responded well rather than attacking the person in response;
- work out mutually beneficial solutions.

Learning how to respond well to verbal attacks is an essential skill for every person. Most people do not enjoy verbal assaults. However, you will achieve remarkable success in your life and relationships when you learn how to respond effectively to an angry person.

Responding to confrontation is not easy for most people—even when the confrontation is done well. The principles in this Key will help you respond to any confrontation—done positively or negatively. Since it is more difficult to deal with a verbal attack, this Key focuses mainly on how to deal with confrontations that are not done well.

Criticism is normal in communities—family, church, mission, business, ministry and more. The skills taught in this chapter will help you react in ways leading to resolution whether or not you are at fault and in every relationship in your life.

Proverbs for Receiving Confrontation

The Bible has so much to say about relationships and how to resolve conflict. These Scriptures should provide ample motivation for growing in this area of our lives. As you read each verse, ask yourself the following questions:

1. What do these verses say about how we *should* receive confrontation?

2. What do they say about how we *shouldn't* receive it?

3. How am I most likely to react to a confrontation delivered negatively?

4. What might I need to change in how I react to confrontation?

Proverbs 1:7 (NLT): "Fools despise wisdom and discipline."

Proverbs 1:23 (HCSB): "If you respond to my [wisdom's] warning, then I will pour out my spirit on you and teach you my words."

Proverbs 5:12 (AMP): "You say, how I hated instruction and discipline, and my heart despised reproof!"

Proverbs 9:7–8 (HCSB): "The one who corrects a mocker will bring dishonor on himself; the one who rebukes a wicked man will get hurt. Don't rebuke a mocker, or he will hate you; rebuke a wise man, and he will love you."

Proverbs 10:17 (ESV): "Whoever heeds instruction is on the path to life, but he who rejects reproof leads others astray."

Proverbs 12:1 (NKJV): "Whoever loves instruction loves knowledge, but he who hates correction is stupid."

Proverbs 13:1 (NLT): "A mocker refuses to listen to correction."

Proverbs 13:18 (NLT): "If you ignore criticism, you will end in poverty and disgrace; if you accept correction, you will be honored."

Proverbs 15:5 (AMP): "He who regards reproof acquires prudence."

Proverbs 15:10, 12 (NKJV): "Harsh discipline is for him who forsakes the way, and he who hates correction will die. ... A scoffer does not love one who corrects him, nor will he go to the wise."

Proverbs 15:31–32 (ESV): "The ear that listens to life-giving reproof will dwell among the wise. Whoever ignores instruction despises himself, but he who listens to reproof gains intelligence."

Proverbs 17:10 (NKJV): "Rebuke is more effective for a wise man than a hundred blows on a fool."

Proverbs 19:25 (NIV): "Rebuke the discerning, and they will gain knowledge."

Proverbs 29:1 (NIV): "Whoever remains stiff-necked after many rebukes will suddenly be destroyed—without remedy."

How to Respond to Verbal Attacks

There are many ways to respond to an attack. Some are positive and improve the relationship. Others are negative and hurt the relationship.

When someone verbally attacks you, your first task is to try to lower the person's anger level so you can begin to resolve the problem. Be realistic. An appropriate response doesn't guarantee the person's anger will calm down, but it greatly increases the probability.

It is easier to respond well when someone confronts you respectfully and gently. But when attacked or confronted poorly, you may be tempted to respond in kind. Your anger, hurt or defensiveness may take over and control your responses before you even realize what is happening. But you can learn new patterns!

To respond well to attacks
- Eliminate poor reactions.
- Learn appropriate responses.

- Commit to God to respond in appropriate ways.
- Rely on God for the power to respond appropriately.

When attacked with words, your response will affect the outcome. If you respond with anger, negotiations will break down and you will not come to a win/win solution. However, when you respond in the ways this Key suggests, most of the time you will have amicable outcomes.

Many people lack the confidence and the skills to accept poorly delivered confrontation in a positive way. To learn successful strategies to deactivate an explosive situation or defuse a burst of anger, you must do the following:

- Discover effective ways to avoid inflaming a situation into an argument.
- Direct disagreements or misunderstandings toward consensus, compromise and understanding.
- Apply the tools needed to resolve the negative verbal challenge.
- Guide an angry confrontation toward a positive outcome.

Review "Some Ways of Defusing Resistance in Conflict" in Chapter 3. These can also help defuse anger when you are being attacked.

Next, let's look at ten powerful ways from Scripture that you can use to defuse a verbal attack.

Ten Biblical Ways to Defuse an Attack

Here are a few of the strategies in Scripture for responding to an attack. These are intended to give you a few initial ideas.

1. **Keep silent**. When someone verbally attacks you, do not interrupt or try to defend yourself. Keep quiet, but let him know you are listening. See Key #2 in *Boost Your Relationship IQ* for more ideas on silence and listening. Consider these questions:

   - How well do you use silence when you are being attacked?

   - How could you use silence more effectively?

   What do these verses say to you?

   Proverbs 11:12 (ESV): "Whoever belittles his neighbor lacks sense, but a man of understanding remains silent."

111

Isaiah 53:7 (NIV): "[The Messiah] was oppressed and afflicted, yet he did not open his mouth; he was led like a lamb to the slaughter, and as a sheep before its shearers is silent, so he did not open his mouth."

John 19:9 (ESV): "[Pilate] entered his headquarters again and said to Jesus, 'Where are you from?' But Jesus gave him no answer."

2. **Think before you react**. When verbally attacked, it is normal to react with anger. However, this only worsens the conflict. Think about what would be the best ways to respond.

   • How might thinking before you react improve the situation when you are attacked?

   • How could you use this strategy more effectively?

   What do these verses say to you?

   Proverbs 15:28 (NKJV): "The heart of the righteous studies how to answer, but the mouth of the wicked pours forth evil."

   Proverbs 29:20 (NLT): "There is more hope for a fool than for someone who speaks without thinking."

   James 1:19–20 (ESV): "Know this, my beloved brothers: let every person be quick to hear, slow to speak, slow to anger; for the anger of man does not produce the righteousness of God."

3. **Actively listen**. Once the person slows down, try to rephrase what you heard so he knows you heard him correctly. Make sure you are using appropriate body language to show you are listening. Even if you do not agree with him, try to understand his perspective.

- How can active listening improve the situation when you are attacked?

- How could you use active listening more effectively?

What do these verses say to you?

Proverbs 19:20 (NIV): "Listen to advice and accept discipline, and at the end you will be counted among the wise."

Proverbs 18:13 (NIV): "To answer before listening—that is folly and shame."

4. **Respond calmly and gently**. No matter how the other person confronts you, use soft words and a gentle tone of voice to state your point of view. Regardless of how you may feel, don't react in anger. When you respond with gentleness, he will probably begin to calm down too.

    You cannot control the feelings of others or force them to respond appropriately. However, responding with gentleness can help to defuse their anger. On the other hand, responding with anger increases the other person's antagonism.

    - When attacked, how will responding calmly and gently improve the situation?

    - How could you use this strategy more effectively?

    What do these verses say to you?

    Proverbs 15:1 (NLT): "A gentle answer deflects anger, but harsh words make tempers flare."

Proverbs 16:21 (ESV): "The wise of heart is called discerning, and sweetness of speech increases persuasiveness."

Proverbs 25:15 (CJB): "With patience a ruler may be won over, and a gentle tongue can break bones."

5. **Agree**. Seek to clarify the facts. Before responding to the attack, seek to understand where the person is coming from and identify the real issue. Anything you can agree with will help defuse his anger so you can come to a positive resolution:
   - Agree with what you can agree with.
   - Agree with whatever you know is true.
   - Agree in principle.
   - Agree with the possibility of truth. Even if you believe he is wrong, you can agree that he *might be right*.

   Consider these questions:
   - How do you think agreeing with the person might improve the situation when you are attacked?

   - How could you use this strategy more effectively?

   What do these verses say to you?

   Matthew 5:25 (ESV): "Come to terms quickly with your accuser while you are going with him to court, lest your accuser hand you over to the judge, and the judge to the guard, and you be put in prison."

   John 18:37 (NLT): "Pilate said, 'So you are a king?' Jesus responded, 'You say I am a king. Actually, I was born and came into the world to testify to the truth. All who love the truth recognize that what I say is true.'"

6. **Give caring feedback**. Let the person know how what he said affects you. However, make sure you do not attack him when you tell him how his words or actions affected you. You might also gently tell him how he could have approached you differently so the interaction would not have been so filled with tension.

- How do you think giving caring feedback might improve relationships when you are attacked?

- How could you use this strategy more effectively?

What do these verses say to you?

> John 19:11 (NIV): "Jesus answered, 'You would have no power over me if it were not given to you from above. Therefore the one who handed me over to you is guilty of a greater sin.'"

> 1 Peter 3:9 (ESV): "Do not repay evil for evil or reviling for reviling, but on the contrary, bless, for to this you were called, that you may obtain a blessing."

7. **Say something kind to the person**. Thank the person for sharing with you. Let him know you value his input and you want to grow. You may also want to tell him how you plan to take action as a result of what he said. If appropriate, consider telling him that you welcome his comments on other issues.

- How do you think saying something kind might improve the situation when you are attacked?

- How could you use this strategy more effectively?

What do these verses say to you?

> Luke 6:28 (NIV): "Bless those who curse you, pray for those who mistreat you."

Romans 12:14 (NLT): "Bless those who persecute you. Don't curse them; pray that God will bless them."

8. **Avoid quarreling**. Arguing will only result in an impasse, increase the person's anger, and possibly cause a complete breakdown in your relationship.

   • How do you think avoiding a quarrel might calm the person who is attacking you?

   • How could you use this strategy more effectively?

   What do these verses say to you?

   Proverbs 17:14 (ESV): "The beginning of strife is like letting out water, so quit before the quarrel breaks out."

   Ephesians 4:31 (NIV): "Get rid of all bitterness, rage and anger, brawling and slander, along with every form of malice."

9. **Offer to help**. Ask the person what he would like you to do now as well as in the future. Let him know you want to repair your relationship and make things right if possible. If appropriate, ask if there is anything else you have done that bothers him.

   • How do you think offering to help might improve your relationship after you have been attacked?

   • How could you use this strategy more effectively?

What do these verses say to you?

> Matthew 5:40–41 (NLT): "If you are sued in court and your shirt is taken from you, give your coat, too. If a soldier demands that you carry his gear for a mile, carry it two miles."

> Luke 6:27 (NLT): "To you who are willing to listen, I say, love your enemies! Do good to those who hate you."

10. **Ask for forgiveness**. Seek forgiveness for anything you may have done wrong, both in the issue you were confronted about and in any ways you may have responded poorly to the confrontation.

   • How do you think asking for forgiveness might improve relationships after you have been attacked?

   • How could you use this strategy more effectively?

What do these verses say to you?

> 1 Samuel 15:24–30 (ESV): "Saul said to Samuel, 'I have sinned, for I have transgressed the commandment of the LORD and your words, because I feared the people and obeyed their voice. Now therefore, please pardon my sin and return with me that I may bow before the LORD.' And Samuel said to Saul, 'I will not return with you. For you have rejected the word of the LORD, and the LORD has rejected you from being king over Israel.' As Samuel turned to go away, Saul seized the skirt of his robe, and it tore. And Samuel said to him, 'The LORD has torn the kingdom of Israel from you this day and has given it to a neighbor of yours, who is better than you. And also the Glory of Israel will not lie or have regret, for he is not a man, that he should have regret.' Then he said, 'I have sinned; yet honor me now before the elders of my people and before Israel, and return with me, that I may bow before the LORD your God.'"

1 Samuel 25:28 (NLT): "Please forgive me if I have offended you in any way. The LORD will surely reward you with a lasting dynasty, for you are fighting the LORD's battles. And you have not done wrong throughout your entire life."

Matthew 5:23–24 (NIV): "If you are offering your gift at the altar and there remember that your brother or sister has something against you, leave your gift there in front of the altar. First go and be reconciled to them; then come and offer your gift."

Conclusion

When someone is angry enough to verbally attack you, there are three possibilities:

- **You may be misunderstood**. Once you help the person calm down, you will be able to seek to resolve any misperceptions.
- **You may be at fault**. At those times, do whatever it takes to make things right with the person.
- **You may be completely innocent**. The other person blames you or may be having a bad day. When you are giving caring feedback, share your perspective on what happened.

In each situation, your response determines the outcome. Many times neither the attacker nor the person attacked are completely blameless.

If you can't resolve the situation quickly, you may want to table it, and then work on resolution later. As you learn to respond in ways to defuse the situation, your relationships will be strengthened.

Recognize that verbal attacks are normal in life. Be prepared. Learn the necessary skills so you will be ready to respond appropriately the next time you are attacked.

If you don't have a plan, you will react in your usual ways.

Think about the following:

1. How would you normally respond if you are verbally attacked?

2. How might your typical response affect your life and communities?

3. How could you respond better?

4. How might responding more effectively affect your relationships?

Questions for Personal or Group Study

Consider the following alone or with a group:

1. Review this Key.

   a. What stands out for you?

   b. Write down any areas in which you need to improve. What will you do to grow in each area?

2. Look back over the "Proverbs for Receiving Confrontation."

   a. Pick two or three of the verses that talk about receiving confrontation *well* to meditate on. What is God saying to you through each one?

b. Pick two or three of the verses on receiving confrontation *poorly* to meditate on. What is God saying to you through them?

c. Based on these verses, what might you need to do differently the next time you are confronted in anger?

3. Reflect on the last time you were verbally attacked. Write your answers.
   a. Why were you attacked?

   b. How did you respond?

   c. What was the result of the confrontation?

   d. Were you satisfied with the result? Why or why not?

   e. If you were not happy with the outcome of the attack, what could you have done differently to change the outcome? Note: You may want to review this question after you finish this Key.

4. Think about likely scenarios in which people might attack you in your communities (these could include past experiences you've had). What would be the best ways to respond to each situation? Go through this list of relationships, thinking of times or situations that have caused or might spark an attack:

a. Spouse or other family member

b. Boss or employee

c. Someone in your mission

d. Who else?

5. Here are a few biblical commands on how to respond to those who treat us poorly. As you look at them, consider these things:

a. Think back on the last time you were mistreated.

b. How did your response compare to these commands?

c. Write out one or two possible responses about how you might react the next time you are treated poorly.

Matthew 5:38–41 (NIV): "You have heard that it was said, 'Eye for eye, and tooth for tooth.' But I tell you, do not resist an evil person. If anyone slaps you on the right cheek, turn to them the other cheek also. And if anyone wants to sue you and take your shirt, hand over your coat as well. If anyone forces you to go one mile, go with them two miles."

Luke 6:27–31 (ESV): "I say to you who hear, Love your enemies, do good to those who hate you, bless those who curse you, pray for those who abuse you. To one who strikes you on the cheek, offer the other also, and from one who takes away your cloak do not withhold your tunic either. Give to everyone who begs from you, and from one who takes away your goods do not demand them back. And as you wish that others would do to you, do so to them."

6. Review the "Ten Biblical Ways to Defuse an Attack."

   a. Which are the most difficult for you?

   b. Which are easiest for you?

   c. Consider memorizing this list so you are prepared the next time you are attacked.

   d. Talk with a friend or partner about which of these you need to work on. Talk through the questions with each point.

   e. Discuss with a friend what you learned from the verses.

   f. Prayerfully consider which you want to practice in your responses when you are confronted poorly.

A Verse to Meditate On and Memorize

Choose a verse from this chapter. If you are not sure which to choose, try this one:

Proverbs 29:11 (NIV): "Fools give full vent to their rage, but the wise bring calm in the end."

Snapshots

Go to the section titled "Snapshots" to record points you want to remember and/or do.

Chapter 11

How Do I Respond to Verbal Attacks?

Bless those who persecute you; bless and do not curse.
Romans 12:14 NKJV

In this chapter you'll use these tools to assess how you are doing when you are verbally attacked:

- A self-assessment to rate how you are currently doing
- A chance to evaluate your core beliefs about verbal attacks
- Two hypothetical scenarios for you to consider how you would normally react and how you might react better

How Do I Respond When I Am Verbally Attacked?

Consider how you are doing at receiving confrontation. Evaluate both how you are doing with family or people close to you versus other people in your life. Use this scale to indicate your responses.

1 = Hardly ever, 2 = Occasionally, 3 = Sometimes,
4 = Often, 5 = Nearly always

Family Others

_____ _____ 1. I avoid interrupting and remain silent until the person stops talking.

_____ _____ 2. When I am confronted about a problem, I don't become defensive, even when the person confronts me in anger.

_____ _____ 3. I use my best listening skills with the person confronting me.

_____ _____ 4. Even if the person confronting me is attacking me, I do not let him control my responses.

_____ _____ 5. I keep in mind that my first responsibility is to glorify God in the way I respond.

_____ _____ 6. Before responding, I ask for clarification of the facts and try to understand the issue from the other person's point of view.

_____ _____ 7. When I state my point of view, I do it calmly and gently, no matter how the other person is acting.

_____ _____ 8. When the timing is right, I ask for permission to state my point of view.

_____ _____ 9. If the other person is feeling hurt, offended or angry, I try to empathize.

_____ _____ 10. I express my need and desire for forgiveness if I have hurt or wronged the person.

_____ _____ 11. I offer to help the person in ways I can legitimately do so.

_____ _____ 12. I agree with whatever truth there may be in the confrontation.

_____ _____ 13. I avoid quarreling no matter how much the person wants to argue.

_____ _____ 14. I respond in a loving way regardless of the other person's behavior.

_____ _____ 15. If I believe the person is sinning in the way he is confronting me, I prayerfully consider whether to confront the sin or to overlook it.

Look over your responses to "How Do I Respond When I Am Verbally Attacked?"

1. Congratulate yourself! Did you score a 4 or a 5 in any of the statements above? If so, you are doing great!

2. Needs Improvement. Prayerfully consider each of your 1s and 2s.

    a. Write an action plan to improve each area of concern.

b. Choose one or two to begin working on right now.

c. Once you have improved the 1s and 2s, work on the 3s.

3. Talk with someone who will hold you accountable.

a. With whom will you talk?

b. When will you call?

Core Beliefs

Core Belief #1

*When I am attacked, my first responsibility is to respond in
ways that will glorify God.*

First Corinthians 10:31 (NIV) says, "Whether you eat or drink or whatever
you do, do it all for the glory of God."

When someone confronts you in anger, your first task is to respond
in ways that help calm his anger. To hold this core belief doesn't mean
you respond well in every situation, but that you are committed to *trying to*
always respond well.

Think about this core belief, then answer these questions:

1. How can responding appropriately to verbal attacks build relationships
   in your community?

2. When you are attacked, how do you normally act?

3. If you are tempted to respond angrily, can you afford to continue acting
   this way? Why or why not?

4. What could you change in relation to this core belief that will help your communities?

Core Belief #2

I am only accountable for my response and cannot control others.

You can't control the feelings of others or force them to respond appropriately.

Romans 12:18 (NIV) says, "If it is possible, as far as it depends on you, live at peace with everyone." It's not always possible; but when you respond in godly ways, you significantly increase the probability that the other person will calm down and will be able to deal with the issues at hand. Then you can have a win/win solution. However, you must come to grips with the fact that sometimes, no matter what you do, the other person may not respond well. Your responsibility is to respond appropriately. You are *not* responsible for the other person's response.

Think about this core belief. Then answer these questions:

1. Consider this: nothing always works. In other words, you may do very well in responding in godly ways, but the other person may still not be willing to give up his wrath.

2. What do you think about Core Belief #2?

3. Are you willing to apply this chapter's principles, even though they may not always work? Why or why not?

4. What will you do when you use the principles in this course, but they don't work in a given situation?

As I was finalizing this book, I had an opportunity to practice the principles. I was staying with close friends in another city when the husband's rage came against me. I had simply expressed my disagreement with what someone else thought should be included in this book. When I tried to talk to my friend, he got further enraged. Despite trying to apply the principles in this book, nothing I did could lower his anger. He threatened me and threw me out of his house, not even allowing me to retrieve all my things.

I was amazed at my feelings. I experienced no fear or anger, only grief for him and his family, as well as my broken relationship with them. (It wasn't what I wanted, but in his rage, he said I was never to see him or his family again.) I felt sadness for him, because he doesn't understand how much God loves him or how much I love them. I continue to pray for them daily.

Hypothetical Scenarios

Read through these real-life situations. Then answer the questions following each.

Single Mom is Angry Because Everything Is about Couples. After a missions team meeting, a single mom, Margaret, comes up to you very angry. She has faithfully been a part of the team for the past two years and gotten involved in many areas. She has always been pleasant to talk with; however, today she is livid. She is angry because she says everything is always about couples, never about singles or single parents. She feels like she doesn't belong in this mission because no one seems to acknowledge her situation. Instead, everyone only seems to address issues for married couples.

1. How would you normally respond to this situation?

2. What have you learned from this Key to help you respond better to this situation?

3. Look back over "Ten Biblical Ways to Defuse an Attack" in Chapter 10. Which of them would be hardest for you to implement in this situation?

4. How can you prepare yourself to handle a situation like this?

5. What do you think the outcome might be if you respond to Margaret according to the guidelines in this Key?

6. What do you think the outcome might be if you respond in anger and lash back at her?

Angry Contractor. You hired Randy to do work on a home you purchased. Your contract with him says you will pay him $300 at the beginning, $300 when he is halfway through and the balance when the job is completed. He still has a significant amount of work left to do. You have already paid him $700—this is more than you agreed on before the job was complete. Although you realize you probably should have stuck to your contract, you gave him extra because he appeared to need it.

Yesterday, he asked you for additional money. You said you couldn't pay him any extra until the job was completed. Today, when you show up at the job site, you are met with a barrage of angry words. He demands $1000 today for his recent work, even though he still has a lot to finish. He threatens to sue you, and uses some of the foulest language you've ever heard. What would you do?

1. How would you normally respond to this situation?

2. What have you learned from this Key to help you respond better when you are being attacked verbally?

3. Which of the "Ten Biblical Ways to Defuse an Attack" in Chapter 10 would be hardest for you to implement in this situation?

4. How can you prepare yourself to handle a situation like this?

5. What do you think the outcome might be if you respond to your contractor according to the guidelines in this Key?

6. What do you think the outcome might be if you respond in anger and lash back at him?

7. How might you respond differently if you were at fault? Perhaps you were supposed to pay him his second installment, but you forgot.

Inviting Confrontation

Inviting constructive criticism or feedback is an excellent way to open up communication and build trust. It may be frightening, but it can actually reduce your fear and defensiveness. You might want to consider asking people you trust to confront you, those who are not likely to do it in anger.

1. Invite one or two close friends or coworkers to feel free to talk to you whenever there is something they disagree with, or think you need to be confronted about.

2. You might want to invite your supervisor or those whom you supervise to talk to you when they disagree with you.

3. Ask those you invited to confront you whenever they notice you say or do things that hurt them or others.

4. Make a commitment to yourself to respond in appropriate ways whenever confronted.

5. List individuals you will invite to confront you and when you will ask them.

Questions for Personal or Group Study

Consider the following alone or with a group:

1. Review this Key.

    a. What stands out for you?

    b. Write down any areas in which you need to improve. What will you do to grow in each area?

2. Consider Jesus' example in the following verses. What can you learn about responding well as you think about His responses?

    Luke 22:70 (ESV): "They all said, 'Are you the Son of God, then?' And he said to them, 'You say that I am.'"

    Luke 23:34 (NLT): "Jesus said, 'Father, forgive them, for they don't know what they are doing.'"

    1 Peter 2:21–23 (NKJV): "To this you were called, because Christ also suffered for us, leaving us an example, that you should follow His steps: 'who committed no sin, nor was deceit found in His mouth'; who, when He was reviled, did not revile in return; when He suffered, He did not threaten, but committed Himself to Him who judges righteously."

3. Look over your responses to the self-assessment at the beginning of this chapter. Reexamine any issues in which you responded with a score of three or less. Decide which ones you want to grow in, and what you will begin doing differently. Share with someone who will hold you accountable.

4. Reflect and ask yourself:
   - From whom in my life am I having the most difficulty receiving confrontation?

   - What do I believe are the reasons it is so difficult?

   - Decide how you can respond differently the next time you are confronted by him, and make a commitment to do so.

5. Go over this Key with your staff or team. Discuss how well you're doing and any changes you want to make as a group and/or individually. Make a commitment to lovingly receive confrontation from each other.

6. Talk with your spouse or a close friend:
   - "What would you like me to do differently when you confront me?"

   - "One thing I would like to do differently when you confront me is ..."

- "How can we change the ways we confront each other so it will be easier to receive?"

7. For parents or others in leadership, do the following:
   - Consider: "What do I want to begin doing differently when my children (or those under my leadership) confront me?"

   - Ask them, including children six years old or older: "What would you like me to do differently when you talk to me about something you don't like?"

   - Consider areas in which you would like to invite them to confront you. Then invite them to do so.

A Verse to Meditate On and Memorize

Choose a verse from this chapter. If you are not sure which to choose, try this one:

Romans 12:14 (NKJV): "Bless those who persecute you; bless and do not curse."

Snapshots

Go to the section titled "Snapshots" to record points you want to remember and/or do.

Chapter 12

How Can I Respond Better When I'm Attacked?

You have heard that it was said, "Eye for eye, and tooth for tooth."
But I tell you, do not resist an evil person.
If anyone slaps you on the right cheek, turn to them the other cheek also.
And if anyone wants to sue you and take your shirt, hand over your coat as well.
If anyone forces you to go one mile, go with them two miles.
Matthew 5:38–41 NIV

In this chapter, you will do these activities:

1. Observe two skill demonstrations[1] with a friend, coworker or family member who also wants to develop the skills.

    a. The first shows positive ways to respond to a verbal attack.

    b. The second shows what happens if you respond in similar ways as the attacker.

2. Write down your observations of the skill in action.

3. Take turns practicing responding to verbal attacks.

4. Review what you learned from role-playing the skill.

As you watch the demonstrations, consider the following:

1. The people demonstrating the skill may not handle the situation like you would—watch for the principles you discovered in this Key.

2. You can apply everything you see. Remember, you don't have to be a trained counselor.

---

1 You can get access to the demonstrations at http://rddemos.rrbooks.org.

3. Avoid getting caught up in the issue they are dealing with.

Ten Biblical Ways to Defuse an Attack

As you watch the demonstrations and when you practice, keep this list with you to remind you of what to do:

1. Keep silent.
2. Think before you react.
3. Actively listen.
4. Respond calmly and gently.
5. Agree.
6. Give caring feedback.
7. Say something kind to the person.
8. Avoid quarreling.
9. Offer to help.
10. Ask for forgiveness.

Demonstration #1: How to Respond to Verbal Attacks

Watch this demonstration showing many ways of defusing an attack. As you watch, consider the following:

1. Rather than focusing on what the attacker is saying and doing, focus on what the person being attacked says and does. Remember, his words and manners may be very different from yours.

2. As you watch the demonstration, write down how the person being attacked defuses the attacker's anger, using this chart:

Verbally	Nonverbally

After the demonstration, talk with your practice partner about the following:

1. What did the person being attacked *say* that was helpful in his confrontation?

2. What did he *do* that was helpful?

3. What would you do differently in this situation?

4. What did you learn from watching the demonstration that can help you in real life?

Demonstration #2: How NOT to Respond to Verbal Attacks

Watch the second demonstration on how *not* to respond to an attack. Notice how different the situation is when you respond in the same way as the person who is attacking you. Talk with your role-play partner or write down:

1. What differences did you see between the two demonstrations?

2. What do you think the result of the second role play will be?

3. What kind of resolution do you think they will have?

Practice

Here is your opportunity to practice this skill in a safe environment. Practicing improves your skills and increases your confidence when you are faced with a real attack. It is much better to practice how to respond to verbal attacks in a safe environment than to "practice" it with an angry person.

Set Up and Practice

1. Choose a situation to practice from this list:

   a. The same situation you saw demonstrated

   b. A real situation you experienced

   c. One of the hypothetical scenarios from Chapter 11

2. One person attacks the other. The person attacking should be as angry and defensive as possible, but let the anger subside after a while. If the "attacker" is not angry enough, it will not give the other person a good opportunity to practice this skill.

3. The person being attacked should respond as well as possible, using the skills learned in this chapter.

4. Then trade roles so you both have a chance to practice.

After You Practice

Talk about:

1. What did you learn from the practice?

2. What will you do differently in real life?

3. What areas do you need to work on to improve how you respond to verbal attacks?

Questions for Personal or Group Study

Consider the following alone or with a group:

1. Review this Key.

    a. What stands out for you?

    b. Write down any areas in which you need to improve. What will you do to grow in each area?

2. What can you learn from these verses?

    Romans 12:14 (NLT): "Bless those who persecute you. Don't curse them; pray that God will bless them."

    Romans 12:17–19 (NKJV): "Repay no one evil for evil. Have regard for good things in the sight of all men. If it is possible, as much as depends on you, live peaceably with all men. Beloved, do not avenge yourselves, but rather give place to wrath; for it is written, 'Vengeance is Mine, I will repay,' says the Lord."

    1 Peter 3:9 (NIV): "Do not repay evil with evil or insult with insult. On the contrary, repay evil with blessing, because to this you were called so that you may inherit a blessing."

3. Go over this Key with someone in your community.
    - Discuss how well each of you are applying these skills in your community.
    - Discuss what, if any, changes you want to make.
    - Talk about, "One thing I would like to do differently when I am confronted is …"

4. Consider the following:

   • How can I prepare myself for a verbal attack?

   • What do I need to do differently when I'm attacked?

   • Write down specific strategies you will use.

5. Practice the skills in this chapter several times with your role-play partner or with different people. Practice does help you learn how to respond better in a real situation.

A Verse to Meditate On and Memorize

Choose a verse from this chapter. If you are not sure which to choose, try these:

> Matthew 5:38–41 (NIV): "You have heard that it was said, 'Eye for eye, and tooth for tooth.' But I tell you, do not resist an evil person. If anyone slaps you on the right cheek, turn to them the other cheek also. And if anyone wants to sue you and take your shirt, hand over your coat as well. If anyone forces you to go one mile, go with them two miles."

Snapshots

Go to the section titled "Snapshots" to record points you want to remember and/or do.

Strategy for Success

This is your opportunity to look at a situation in your life you haven't yet resolved or may not have resolved well. You can evaluate how you responded when someone confronted you in anger and what you may need to do differently in the future.

1. Write a brief account of a past or present situation.

2. What have you learned from this Key that could help you resolve future conflicts?

3. Prayerfully consider which principles in this Key could be a catalyst for your future growth.

Key #4 Facilitate Peace

What do you do when two people you know are in conflict with each other and can't work it out themselves? This Key examines two powerful tools you can use to help resolve conflict between other people. Learning how to use these tools effectively will not only leave you better equipped for conflicts between loved ones, but it will prepare you for powerful ministry opportunities and helping others in your mission or community with conflicts.

Great rewards come from being able to help bring people through conflict to restoration of a relationship.

Chapter 13

One on One

Blessed are the peacemakers, for they will be called children of God.
Matthew 5:9 NIV

Jack had been angry with his mom for years. Instead of talking with her, he stayed away from her and often kept her from seeing her grandkids.

I talked with each of them separately and discovered they both longed for a good relationship with the other but neither thought it was possible. I worked with each individually and then invited both of them to my house and facilitated their talking. It was amazing to watch them begin to talk about how they were feeling and see the other one acknowledge those feelings.

When you have walked through the process to manage your own conflict, you can become a catalyst to help others manage their conflicts. You'll learn how to work with just one person or mediate between two people who are in a conflict. Are you saying, "I'm not a trained counselor; I can't do this"? Yes, you can. This section guides you through a process to effectively help other people.

Helping others manage conflicts is a vital way to minister to them. In Philippians 4:3, Paul asked a leader to help two women who were struggling in their relationship: "I ask you also, true companion, help these women, who have labored side by side with me in the gospel together with Clement and the rest of my fellow workers, whose names are in the book of life" (ESV).

This is a complex process which requires our best helping skills. As a friend or leader, you no doubt have opportunities to intervene when others have unresolved conflicts in their relationships. You may choose to help the person who comes to you or work with both parties together. In this chapter, we will look at both situations, starting with working with one person.

Prepare Yourself to Help Others with Conflict

Before you can help others, you need to consider these things:

Your Attitudes

Your own attitudes toward conflict will partly determine your effectiveness in helping others. If you didn't do it earlier, take the self-assessment, "How Am I at Managing My Conflicts?" in Chapter 4. If you did do it, review your answers. Obviously, this cannot adequately measure your attitudes; but it might give you a general idea of how healthy your attitudes are toward conflict.

1. List attitudes you may need to work on.

2. How will you begin to work on each one?

3. Write out a specific plan of action.

Crusty and Tender Feelings

Feelings play a critical role in conflict resolution. As we saw in Chapter 3, "crusty" feelings such as anger, fury, exasperation and frustration often surface in a conflict. But these repel the other person and make it very difficult to respond with empathy. Crusty feelings make a poor basis for conflict resolution.

Underneath those harsh emotions almost always lay "tender" feelings such as hurt, disappointment, sadness, loneliness and feeling unimportant. If you can listen in a caring way and patiently draw out these tender feelings from each other, you'll draw closer and be much more motivated to resolve your conflicts.

Before you begin working with anyone in conflict, you must be aware of the difference between these two types of feelings. People usually come to a confrontation expressing crusty feelings. Your job is to help them get down to the tender feelings so resolution can occur.

Prepare to Listen to One Side

At times you may observe unresolved issues between friends and coworkers. Or a person may come to discuss a conflict with someone else. In both situations you have a unique opportunity to help. The Lord may lead you to intervene and thus be a powerful catalyst in resolving the conflict. Make sure the Holy Spirit is leading you and you are not getting involved because you have a need to fix people.

Let's look at a few issues to consider when interacting with only one of the individuals involved in an unresolved conflict.

Objectives

1. Your immediate purpose is to give the person an opportunity to talk out the conflict situation in a safe, nonjudgmental environment.

2. Your long-range purpose is to facilitate resolution and reconciliation. You might go through the "Conflict Management Checklist" in Chapter 4 with the person.

Advantages of Listening to One Side

1. It may help him to express his feelings as you use your best listening skills.

2. Talking will help him sort out feelings, facts and misbeliefs.

3. You can encourage him to take steps to resolve the conflict and forgive the other person.

Dangers of Listening to One Side

1. You may become angry yourself at the other party. Proverbs 18:17 (NIV) says, "In a lawsuit the first to speak seems right, until someone comes forward and cross-examines."

2. You might play "ain't it awful" and aggravate the problem. You could make the person angrier if you seem to agree that he is right and the other person is totally wrong.

3. He may think you agree with him as you use good listening skills, or you may actually take his side.

4. You may participate in gossip if the person only wants to tell how bad the other person is and doesn't want help.

5. You may get a skewed view of the situation when you only hear one side

Steps to Take to Help One Person

The particular steps depend on the situation, but these often help:

Step 1: As the person begins to share, try to determine as soon as possible what he has done to try to resolve the issue with the other person. If he hasn't talked with the other person, your first responsibility is to urge him do so.

Step 2: Listen well. Give nonverbal acknowledgment showing you are listening, such as eye contact or nodding your head.

Proverbs 18:2 (NIV): "Fools find no pleasure in understanding but delight in airing their own opinions."

Proverbs 18:13 (ESV): "If one gives an answer before he hears, that is folly and shame."

Step 3: Draw him out, especially his emotions, regarding the facts as he sees them.

Step 4: As you listen, it is usually best to remain neutral. Remember you are hearing his perceptions.

Step 5: Ask questions to help him see things more clearly, or to gently confront him with faulty perceptions and judgments.

Proverbs 25:12 (ESV): "Like a gold ring or an ornament of gold is a wise reprover to a listening ear."

Step 6: Encourage him to go again to the person to try to resolve the conflict.

If he has tried and failed, or is too afraid to go back alone, you might offer to go with him.

If he is willing to go, give him ideas on how to confront the issue.

Offer to role-play the conflict with him.

Proverbs 20:18 (NIV) says, "Plans are established by seeking advice; so if you wage war, obtain guidance."

Step 7: Inspire him to review the principles in Key #1 in this book to provide ideas on how to deal with this conflict.

Step 8: If this doesn't resolve the issue, offer to work with both parties as a mediator.

Core Belief about Helping One Side Manage a Conflict

Remember: A core belief is a firmly held conviction that consistently motivates behavior.

Belief + Consistent Action = Core Belief

Core Belief

I don't have to be a trained mediator to help people in conflict.

Anyone can learn to help someone in conflict with another person. While you don't have to be a counselor, you do need to develop and practice the skills in this chapter to become comfortable implementing them.

Think about this core belief and answer these questions:

1. What does it mean to you in life and relationships?

2. What might you need to do to experience success in helping others?

3. What might be the most difficult part for you when helping others who are in conflict?

Questions for Personal or Group Study

Consider the following alone or with a group:

1. Review this Key.

   a. What stands out for you?

   b. Write down any areas in which you need to improve. What will you do to grow in each area?

2. What can you learn about helping others manage conflict from these Scriptures?

   Psalm 133:1–2 (NIV): "How good and pleasant it is when God's people live together in unity! It is like precious oil poured on the head, running down on the beard, running down on Aaron's beard, down on the collar of his robe."

   Matthew 5:9 (NKJV): "Blessed are the peacemakers, for they shall be called sons of God."

   Philippians 4:2–3 (NLT): "I appeal to Euodia and Syntyche. Please, because you belong to the Lord, settle your disagreement. And I ask you, my true partner, to help these two women, for they worked hard with me in telling others the Good News."

3. Study "Steps to Take" under "Listening to One Side."

    a. Which would be most difficult for you? Why?

    b. Learn the steps well so you will be ready to use them when opportunities arise.

4. Make a commitment now that when someone begins telling you about a problem they have with another person, you will inquire what he has done to try to resolve it. Then respond according to the "Steps to Take."

A Verse to Meditate On and Memorize

Choose a verse from this chapter. If you are not sure which to choose, try this one:

> Matthew 5:9 (NASB): "Blessed are the peacemakers, for they shall be called sons of God."

Snapshots

Go to the section titled "Snapshots" to record points you want to remember and/or do.

Chapter 14

It Takes Two to Tango but a Dance Coach Is Appreciated

The one who states his case first seems right,
until the other comes and examines him.
Proverbs 18:17 ESV

You will be a great help to both parties if you can facilitate the resolution of their conflict. This takes greater skill than dealing with one person, but the risks are worth the potential outcome.

Note: this chapter talks about having both parties in the same room. You can also do mediation with the two parties in separate rooms, which is much easier. You will use most of the same steps in this chapter. Having them in separate rooms can be better, especially if one of the people is abusive in anyway.

The first time I was in mediation, the mediator refused to make the other person, a fellow missionary, keep the ground rules. I walked out. Later the mediator called me and said I was right to leave, because he wasn't doing his job right. The second time I was in mediation the mediator put us in separate rooms and she went back and forth between the two rooms. That process went well and we were able to come to a mutually agreeable solution. Using separate rooms works very well if there is any abuse in the relationship.

Prepare to Be a Mediator

You do not have to be a trained mediator to help people work through their conflicts. However, you need to do five things:

1. Spend time in prayer and possibly even fasting before you go into a session. Allow the Holy Spirit to lead you.

2. Learn and practice the mediation steps in this chapter to make the process successful.

3. Look for opportunities to practice the skills in this chapter before a real situation comes up.

4. Make a choice to be as unbiased as possible. The mediation process will not work if you are biased for or against either of the parties. If you cannot be objective, then direct the people in conflict to find someone else to mediate.

5. Commit to holding both people to the ground rules you set up. If you don't, then it can become unsafe for one or both of them.

Objectives

1. Provide a safe, controlled situation for expressing facts and feelings.

2. Facilitate the problem-solving process to bring resolution, if possible.

Advantages of Being a Mediator

1. Your presence provides a safe environment for both individuals.

2. They will probably control their emotions and speech better in your presence.

3. You can provide objective direction and guidance in coming to a solution.

4. You may observe and confront destructive behavior.

Dangers of Being a Mediator

1. You can easily take sides or be perceived to be doing so by one or both sides.

2. You might be attacked.

3. You might impose a solution which is not viable. They may seem to agree but possibly won't follow through with it.

Steps to Take to Help Two or More People

Each situation will require its own approach. These steps may help:
Step 1: Lay the foundation.

- Set up the meeting.
- Be sensitive to the timing and location.
- Consider whether beginning the session with prayer will be helpful. For example, if you are working with not-yet-believers, it is probably better to not begin with prayer.
- Ensure both parties are willing to seek a solution.

Step 2: Get agreement on the ground rules. Decide which ones to suggest and see if they agree to them. Once they agree to the ground rules, you need to make sure they follow them. Every time a ground rule is broken, stop the conversation. Gently remind the person who broke the rule of what he did.

For the process to work, it is essential you make sure both parties follow the ground rules. This is one of the most difficult parts of your job as a mediator. Especially at the beginning, one or both parties will usually violate the ground rules. Here are a few possible ground rules:

WHERE ARE YOU?

HEAD LEVEL

FACTS
IDEAS
THOUGHTS

ADVICE
SOLUTIONS
JUDGMENTS

HEART LEVEL

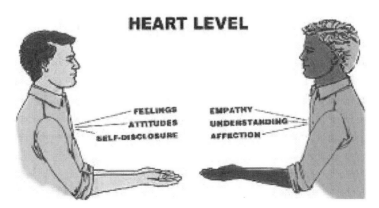

FEELINGS
ATTITUDES
SELF-DISCLOSURE

EMPATHY
UNDERSTANDING
AFFECTION

- Keep to one issue at a time.
- Don't interrupt.
- Restate what you just heard before giving your views.
- Don't attack the other person.

Step 3: Get them talking to each other, not to you, except for discussing the process. Every time they begin to address the issues with you, stop them. Remind them to talk to each other. Encourage and help them to understand each other both on head and heart levels. Look at the picture below to learn about communicating on head and heart levels.

Facilitate by saying, "Before you give your point of view, please put what you just heard into your own words." Then ask the other person, "Is that a true representation of your feelings and the facts?"

Step 4: After both have expressed feelings and facts, help them explore options for a solution. Work toward a win/win solution both parties wholeheartedly accept. To learn about helping people explore options, study Key #5.

Step 5: Make sure they have forgiven each other or are committed to doing so.

Step 6: Help them restore their relationship. Facilitate a conversation between them in which they determine what needs to happen for their relationship to get back on track. Does either of them need to repair any damage done? If so, what needs to be done and when will it happen?

Step 7: Set up a follow-up time to see how things are going.

As both parties begin to understand each other and start communicating, you as the mediator are able to step back more and more. Once their communication becomes effective, your only function is to

- Clarify any questions they have.
- Move them to the next step when they are ready.

Few challenges in life require more of God's wisdom and insight than this. Even though it is difficult, great joy comes from being used by the Lord to help bring people through conflict into loving unity. Psalm 133:1 (NIV) says, "How good and pleasant it is when God's people live together in unity!"

Core Belief about Helping Both Sides Manage a Conflict

Core Belief

Facilitating conflict management between two people takes practice.

This skill in not something you will become good at unless you take the time to practice it in a safe environment.

Think about this core belief and answer these questions:

1. What does this core belief mean to you?

2. Do you agree that facilitating conflict management between two people takes practice? Why or why not?

3. How can you become experienced at this skill? What will you do?

Questions for Personal or Group Study

Consider the following alone or with a group:

1. Review this Key.

   a. What stands out for you?

   b. Write down any areas in which you need to improve. What will you do to grow in each area?

2. Study "Steps to Take to Help Two or More People."

   a. Which would be most difficult for you? Why?

   b. Learn the steps well so you will be ready to use them when opportunities arise.

3. What can you learn from these Scriptures about how Jesus helped others manage conflict?

   Mark 9:33–37 (ESV): "[Jesus and the disciples] came to Capernaum. And when he was in the house he asked them, 'What were you discussing on the way?' But they kept silent, for on the way they had argued with one another about who was the greatest. And he sat down and called the twelve. And he said to them, 'If anyone would be first, he must be last of all and servant of all.' And he took a child and put him in the midst of them, and taking him in his arms, he said to them, 'Whoever receives one such child in my name receives me, and whoever receives me, receives not me but him who sent me.'"

Mark 10:41–45 (NIV): "When the ten [disciples] heard about this, they became indignant with James and John. Jesus called them together and said, 'You know that those who are regarded as rulers of the Gentiles lord it over them, and their high officials exercise authority over them. Not so with you. Instead, whoever wants to become great among you must be your servant, and whoever wants to be first must be slave of all. For even the Son of Man did not come to be served, but to serve, and to give his life as a ransom for many.'"

Luke 9:46–48 (NLT): "His disciples began arguing about which of them was the greatest. But Jesus knew their thoughts, so he brought a little child to his side. Then he said to them, 'Anyone who welcomes a little child like this on my behalf welcomes me, and anyone who welcomes me also welcomes my Father who sent me. Whoever is the least among you is the greatest.'"

A Verse to Meditate On and Memorize

Choose a verse from this chapter. If you are not sure which to choose, try this one:

Proverbs 18:17 (ESV): "The one who states his case first seems right, until the other comes and examines him."

Snapshots

Go to the section titled "Snapshots" to record points you want to remember and/or do.

Chapter 15

How Am I at Helping Others Resolve Conflict?

Make every effort to keep the unity of the Spirit through the bond of peace.
Ephesians 4:3 NIV

In this chapter, you will do two assessments:

1. The first will help you see how you are currently doing at helping people who are in conflict.

2. The second will give you hypothetical scenarios so you can determine how you might normally respond to the situation and how you might need to improve your responses.

How Am I Doing at Helping Others Resolve Conflict?

Consider how you are at helping friends, family and others manage their conflicts. The first questions are about working with one person. The last ones are about working with two or more people. Use this scale to indicate your responses.

*1 = Hardly ever, 2 = Occasionally, 3 = Sometimes,
4 = Often, 5 = Nearly always*

Family Others

____ ____ 1. When anyone shares with me about his conflict with another person, I maintain a neutral position rather than taking sides.

____ ____ 2. When someone wants help in managing a conflict, I find out what he has done to try to resolve it and how he feels about what he tried.

_____ _____ 3. I explore with the person all he has considered doing about the conflict and what he thinks about each possibility.

_____ _____ 4. I avoid giving advice to the person who comes to me about a conflict until I understand the situation well.

_____ _____ 5. I try to help the person who comes to me deal with anger and resentment.

_____ _____ 6. When someone shares with me about his conflict with another person, I try to discern whether he is sharing out of a genuine desire to receive help or because he wants someone to agree that he is right.

_____ _____ 7. If I believe someone is gossiping or slandering another person, I let him know I'm not willing to be a part of that.

_____ _____ 8. If one person needs to go alone to the other person and bring up the conflict, I help him be specific about what he will say, and when, where and how he will do it.

_____ _____ 9. When I am mediating a conflict situation, I lay down ground rules at the beginning and I hold both parties to the rules.

_____ _____ 10. I make it clear I am not going to take sides when I am mediating.

_____ _____ 11. I avoid making judgments about who is right and who is wrong.

_____ _____ 12. When I am mediating, I stop the involved individuals from engaging in destructive words or behavior.

_____ _____ 13. If I sense the people are doing well in managing their conflict I keep silent and let them move ahead without interrupting.

_____ _____ 14. After helping others through a conflict I set up a time to check with them to make sure their solutions are working and reconciliation has taken place.

Look over your responses to "How Am I at Helping Others Resolve Conflict?"

1. Congratulate yourself! Did you score a 4 or a 5 in any of the statements above? If so, you are doing great!

2. Needs Improvement. Prayerfully consider each of your 1s and 2s.

   a. Write an action plan to improve each area of concern.

   b. Choose one or two to begin working on right now.

   c. Once you have improved the 1s and 2s, work on the 3s.

3. Talk with someone who will hold you accountable.

   a. With whom will you talk?

   b. When will you call?

Hypothetical Scenario

Read through this real-life situation. Then answer the questions following it.

Trouble between Coworkers. Susie is on staff in your mission. She comes to you as her supervisor because she is very frustrated with Jacob. They are working on a team, but Susie feels like she is doing all the work and Jacob rarely helps. He lets her come up with all the solutions and then he just agrees with her. He takes equal credit when others on staff acknowledge the great ideas. However, if others are negative about a solution, Jacob tells everyone it was Susie's idea. She is tired of feeling like she is doing everything alone and getting blamed for "bad" ideas. (In addition to coworkers, this could also be two children or a variety of other relationships.)

Look at how you could help one person, Susie:

1. How would you normally respond to this situation?

2. What have you learned from this Key to help you respond better to this situation?

3. Look back over "Steps to Take to Help One Person."

   a. Which would be hardest for you to implement in this situation?

   b. Which would be easiest for you to implement?

4. How can you prepare yourself to handle a situation like this?

5. What do you think the outcome might be if you agree with Susie and just let her vent?

6. What do you think the outcome might be if you use the steps in this Key?

This time let's look at the same scenario as above. However, we'll look at working with both people. You now have both Susie and Jacob in your office. What will you do?

1. How would you normally respond to this situation?

2. What have you learned from this Key to help you respond better to this situation?

3. Look back over "Steps to Take to Help Two or More People."

   a. Which would be hardest for you to implement in this situation?

   b. Which would be easiest for you to implement?

4. How can you prepare yourself to handle a situation like this?

5. What do you think the outcome might be if you take sides with either of them?

6. What might happen if you fail to enforce the ground rules?

7. What do you think the outcome might be if you use the steps in this Key?

Questions for Personal or Group Study

Consider the following alone or with a group:

1. Review this Key.

    a. What stands out for you?

    b. Write down any areas in which you need to improve. What will you do to grow in each area?

2. If you are in a position of authority over others, including your children, be especially aware of opportunities to help them manage their conflicts. This applies to any children over three or four years of age.

    a. You might ask them how they feel about the way you've been responding to them when they have a conflict with each other.

    b. Ask what they would like you to do to help when they are in a conflict.

3. Think about situations where others close to you are not getting along. What concepts from the following verses could you use to help them? Underline the ideas you want to encourage them to do and not to do.

    Proverbs 11:12 (ASV): "He that despiseth his neighbor is void of wisdom; but a man of understanding holdeth his peace."

    Proverbs 29:11 (NIV): "Fools give full vent to their rage, but the wise bring calm in the end."

Romans 12:14–21 (NKJV): "Bless those who persecute you; bless and do not curse. Rejoice with those who rejoice, and weep with those who weep. Be of the same mind toward one another. Do not set your mind on high things, but associate with the humble. Do not be wise in your own opinion. Repay no one evil for evil. Have regard for good things in the sight of all men. If it is possible, as much as depends on you, live peaceably with all men. Beloved, do not avenge yourselves, but rather give place to wrath; for it is written, 'Vengeance is Mine, I will repay,' says the Lord. Therefore 'If your enemy is hungry, feed him; if he is thirsty, give him a drink; for in so doing you will heap coals of fire on his head.' Do not be overcome by evil, but overcome evil with good."

4. Look over your responses in "How Am I at Helping Others Manage Conflicts?"

   a. Re-examine any issues in which you responded with a score of three or less.

   b. Decide which ones you want to grow in, and what you will begin doing differently.

   c. Share with someone who will hold you accountable.

5. Which of the hypothetical scenarios would be most difficult for you— working with one person or with both? Why?

6. What could help you prepare to help others with conflict?

A Verse to Meditate On and Memorize

Choose a verse from this chapter. If you are not sure which to choose, try this one:

Ephesians 4:3 (NIV): "Make every effort to keep the unity of the Spirit through the bond of peace."

Snapshots

Go to the section titled "Snapshots" to record points you want to remember and/or do.

Chapter 16

How Can I Better Facilitate Growth for Others?

Each one of you is part of the body of Christ,
and you were chosen to live together in peace.
So let the peace that comes from
Christ control your thoughts. And be grateful.
Colossians 3:15 CEV

In this chapter, you will have two opportunities to watch videos and then practice the skills.

- The first will be working with one person.
- The second will be working with two or more people.

Working with One Person

In this section, you will do the following:

1. Observe the skill demonstration on helping one person. Watch the video with one or more friends, coworkers or family members who also want to grow in their skills.

2. Write down your observations of the skill in action.

3. Take turns practicing helping others manage a conflict.

4. Review what you learned from role playing the skill.

Demonstration—Listening to One Person's Side

The demonstration shows how to apply the skill of helping one person who is in conflict with someone else. As you watch, keep in mind the following:

1. The people in the video may not handle the situation like you would— watch for the principles you discovered in this chapter.

2. You can apply everything you see. Remember, you don't have to be a trained counselor.

3. Avoid getting caught up in the issue they are dealing with in the video.

As you watch the demo, make note on a separate sheet of how you see the mediator following each step in the process:

1. Determining as soon as possible what attempts he has made to resolve the conflict with the other person

2. Listening well to him

3. Drawing out his emotions regarding the facts as he sees them

4. Remaining neutral as he listens

5. Asking questions to help him see things with greater clarity, or gently confronting him with faulty perceptions and judgments

6. Encouraging him to go to the person to try to resolve the conflict

   a. If he has tried and failed, or is too afraid to go back alone, offering to go with him.

   b. If he is willing to go, giving him ideas on how to confront the issue.

   c. Offering to role play the conflict with him.

7. Inspiring him to study Key #1 in this course to provide ideas on how to deal with this conflict

8. If this doesn't resolve the issue, offering to work with both parties as a mediator

After the demonstration, talk with your partner about the following:

1. What did you observe in the demonstration?

2. What would be the most difficult for you in a real situation?

Practice—Listening to One Person's Side

Steps to Take.

1. Review Chapter 13 on listening to one side.

2. Use a hypothetical conflict situation, or a situation you have experienced. You could use the one from the video or the hypothetical scenario.

3. One person approaches the other for help with a conflict he has with a third person.

4. The second person practices the steps from this chapter. See the list of steps under the demonstration, above.

5. Change roles.

After you practice, talk about what you learned:

1. How did it go?

2. What did the person listening do well?

3. What would you do differently in real life?

4. What was difficult for you in this practice?

Working with Both Sides

In this section, you will do the following:

1. Observe the "Mediating a Conflict" skill demonstration. Watch the video with two or more friends, coworkers or family members who also want to grow in their skills.

2. Write down your observations of the skill in action.

3. Take turns practicing helping others manage a conflict.

4. Review what you learned from role playing the skill.

Demonstration #2—Meditating a Conflict

The demonstration shows how to apply the skill of helping people manage conflict when working with both parties. As you watch, keep these things in mind:

1. The people in the demonstration may not handle the situation like you would—watch for the principles you discovered in this chapter.

2. You can apply everything you see. Remember, you don't have to be a trained counselor.

3. Avoid getting caught up in the issue they are dealing with. Instead, focus on watching the skills that are demonstrated.

As you watch the second demonstration, make note of how you see the mediator following each step in the process:

1. Laying the foundation

2. Obtaining agreement on the ground rules

3. Getting them to talk to each other, not to the mediator, except to discuss the process

4. After both have expressed their feelings and facts, helping them explore options for a solution

5. Making sure they have forgiven each other, or are committed to do so, and their relationship is back on track

6. Helping them restore their relationship

7. Setting up a follow-up time to see how things are going

After you watch the video, talk about the following:

1. What you observed in the demonstration

2. What you each think would be the most difficult for you in a real situation

Practice—Mediating a Conflict

Preparing to practice

1. Find two people who are willing to practice with you. It is best if they first watch the video and read this chapter, so they understand what you are doing.

2. Explain to them:
   - You want to learn to help other people manage conflict.
   - You need them to role-play being in a conflict with each other with you mediating.
   - You don't want them to be easy on you. You want them to break the ground rules several times. However, you don't want them to excessively break the rules. You are trying to set up a real-life practice.

Practice mediating a conflict with two people.

1. Review Chapter 14.

2. Use the same situation you used in listening to one side or choose a different one.

3. Go through each step in the process. See the steps under the demonstration, above.

4. Work to keep the two people following the ground rules. If they get off track, you might need to stop the process and start again where you left off.

After you practice, talk about and/or write your answers:

1. How did the practice go?

2. What did the person mediating the conflict do well?

3. Ask the people who were role playing the conflict what worked and what didn't work for them.

4. What would you do differently in real life?

5. What was difficult for you in this role play?

Questions for Personal or Group Study

Consider the following alone or with a group:

1. Review this Key.

   a. What stands out for you?

   b. Write down any areas in which you need to improve. What will you do to grow in each area?

2. What could you use from these verses to help people who aren't getting along?

   Ephesians 4:25–32 (NIV): "Each of you must put off falsehood and speak truthfully to your neighbor, for we are all members of one body. 'In your anger do not sin': Do not let the sun go down while you are still angry, and do not give the devil a foothold. Anyone who has been stealing must steal no longer, but must work, doing something useful with their own hands, that they may have something to share with those in need. Do not let any unwholesome talk come out of your mouths, but only what is helpful for building others up according to their needs, that it may benefit those who listen. And do not grieve the Holy Spirit of God, with whom you were sealed for the day of redemption. Get rid of all bitterness, rage and anger, brawling and slander, along with every form of malice. Be kind and compassionate to one another, forgiving each other, just as in Christ God forgave you."

Colossians 3:8–9 (NLT): "Now is the time to get rid of anger, rage, malicious behavior, slander, and dirty language. Don't lie to each other, for you have stripped off your old sinful nature and all its wicked deeds."

3. Think about any people you know who have unresolved conflicts. Consider whether you should get involved, offering to help them resolve their issues—either with both parties or with only one.

4. Take time to get familiar with or memorize the steps to take both for helping one person and helping two or more people. Practice both situations another. As you practice, you'll become more comfortable in doing the skills.

A Verse to Meditate On and Memorize

Choose a verse from this chapter. If you are not sure which to choose, try this one:

Colossians 3:15 (CEV): "Each one of you is part of the body of Christ, and you were chosen to live together in peace. So let the peace that comes from Christ control your thoughts. And be grateful."

Snapshots

Go to the section titled "Snapshots" to record points you want to remember and/or do.

Strategy for Success

This is your opportunity to look at a situation in your life when others were in conflict. You can evaluate how you did at helping them and what you may need to do differently in the future.

1.   Write an account of a past or current situation where people you knew were in conflict and needed your help.

2.   What have you learned from this Key that could help you handle other situations like this or resolve this one, if it isn't yet dealt with?

3.   What could give you more success as you reach out to others to facilitate peace?

Key #5: Houston, We Have a Problem

Sometimes people have a conflict within themselves because they have a problem they need to solve. Do people in your sphere of influence ever have issues that need resolution? Are you tired of trying to convince people to do what you think they should? Do *you* have problems you don't know how to solve? This key guides you through a process to empower people to solve their own problems, while strengthening rather than straining your relationships.

This skill can be used with anyone in your communities—friends, spouse, children, coworkers, team, church, mission staff and more.

Proverbs 18:13 (NIV) says, "To answer before listening—that is folly and shame."

Chapter 17

The Doctor Is In

As iron sharpens iron, so one person sharpens another.
Proverbs 27:17 NIV

I almost died a few years ago after I had a serious episode where I became blinded, disoriented, confused and then unconscious. The doctor could not find my pulse. It took me over two months to fully recover. During that time I felt exhausted all the time, had extremely blurry vision and many other symptoms. I struggled to keep my ministry to missionaries going. What if after that episode I had gone in to see my doctor and said, "I don't feel very well. Please give me this medicine to make me feel better"? How much could she have helped me? By the way, she couldn't find anything that explained all the sypmtoms I had.

Once I told my doctor what happened and what my symptoms were, she immediately scheduled me for a series of tests to discover what was wrong. Just as my doctor couldn't begin to help me until she knew what my problem was, so we can't effectively help others with their issues until we understand their problems.

"I'm facing a dilemma. What do you think I should do?" a friend asks. He describes a personal struggle similar to one you went through.

What is your first reaction? If you're normal, you will be tempted to tell how you solved your problem or give advice on how to solve his. At times that is helpful, especially if the problem is a "head-level" issue. But often it is on a "heart level," and the "problem" is only the tip of the iceberg.

Look again at the "Where Are You?" chart that we viewed in Chapter 14. It shows how to recognize if a person is on a head or a heart level and what the appropriate responses are to each.

An example of a heart-level issue is when a friend is sad and discouraged, because his child is making very poor decisions. An example of a head-level issue is when someone comes to you, because you are a computer expert and his computer just crashed. However, he may come to you on a heart-level, because he is frustrated about not being able to use his computer. You may need to first acknowledge how he feels, but ultimately, in that situation, he needs your advice and solutions.

When someone has a heart-level issue, you need your best listening and drawing-out skills to get below the surface and understand the problem as fully as possible. The book and online course *Boost Your Relationship IQ* teach how to understand what level a person is on and respond on the appropriate level. If you haven't studied that course, I encourage you to do so because everything in this course is based on the skills in that one.[1]

Although listening is foundational for effective relationships, listening alone may not be enough. People often want and need practical answers to their difficulties. Once the person feels like you cared enough to listen, he may come to a point where he is ready to look at solutions. If you begin with trying to fix the problem, he probably won't be ready for change.

Advice

When someone comes to you with a heart-level problem, first give him time to express his feelings. Then when he is ready to explore solutions, ask yourself these questions:

- Does he really need my advice?
- Will my suggestions lead to the best resolution?
- Will my opinion help him to mature and better analyze other situations?
- Would it be most valuable to help him look into his options rather than telling him what I think he should do?

Advice is telling another person
- what to do;
- how to think;
- what to feel.

Sometimes advice is helpful if it is a head-level topic. However, the issue is often on a heart level and the dilemma is only the tip of the iceberg. Look at the illustration on the next page. Getting below the surface to the core trouble requires your best listening and drawing-out skills.

---

1 www.rrcourses.com.

If you give advice too soon, it may be of little value, or even harmful, because you will be working with a very small part of the total picture. Remember, as an outsider, you cannot understand the total situation and see the underside of the iceberg. For both of you to gain a more realistic grasp of the total picture, encourage him to talk through the problem in detail.

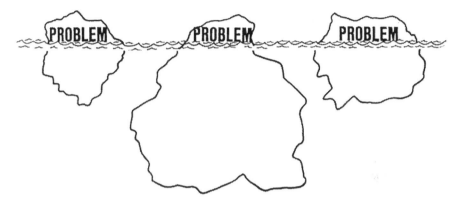

Dangers of Giving Advice

When someone comes to you with a dilemma, are you tempted to give answers based on what you were initially told? Before offering your solutions, consider the following:

- Telling anyone what to do, how to think or what to feel can be helpful—or it can backfire.
- Often an individual shares the surface problem—not the core issue.
- When asked for your opinion, watch and listen for clues—verbal and nonverbal signs—to the person's heart issue.

When anyone shares on a heart level, advice should be your last resort. No matter how much you listen, you can only discern the tip of the iceberg. The person with the problem always knows more than you do.

Advice Can Be a Robber

If used as a substitute for listening, advice robs the other individual of the following:

- true understanding
- feeling cared for
- a safe atmosphere where he can explore his options
- the opportunity to grow in working through struggles
- the chance for the Holy Spirit to give creative resolutions

Giving advice is normal and is often the easiest way for us to deal with someone else's problem because it is usually the quickest. However, it isn't the best way to empower others for lifelong change. Prayerfully consider these questions:

- How do you usually respond when someone comes to you with a problem?

- Is your first response typically to give advice?

- Is there anything you may need to change in the way you help people with problems?

Before You Can Help Others

Before you can help others you may need to do three things. Consider these issues:

Do you need to solve your own problems first? Prayerfully consider whether you are struggling with a situation you haven't resolved. Exploring your options is a productive way to examine, brainstorm and resolve your own difficulties. You can either work through the steps in Chapter 18 with someone you trust or process the steps on your own.

Working through your own problems first helps you understand the process better and gives you practice in solving problems.

Determine if your issues are part of the problem. Before helping others, it is important to resolve your issues first. Rather than being motivated by a healthy and humble desire to minister to others, are you motivated by any of these needs?

- Give advice

- Be needed

- Solve people's problems
- Seek quick solutions

If you answered yes to any of the above, take time to talk to the Lord about them. You might also talk with a godly friend or counselor. Figure out what is causing that motivation. It is probably from a hurt or wounding from your past. For example, recently I realized I grew up feeling like I was not important to anyone. That caused me to have a need to be needed. As a result, I had to work through the hurt that caused me to give advice so I would be needed.

What fears or hurts from the past may hinder you from helping others? Consider and work through the following questions:

- Did you ever try to help someone with a problem and he turned on you?
- Did anyone ever try to control you with his advice?
- Are you afraid you might not have the right solutions, so you don't want to try to help others?
- Did you ever give someone bad advice and it adversely affected him?

If you answered yes to the above questions, how did those situations affect you? How do they hold you back today? What might you need to do to work through them?

Take your hurts and fears to the Lord and allow Him to help you overcome them. You might want to find someone you trust to pray with you and discuss your feelings.

Jesus said in Matthew 7:1, 3, 5 (NIV): "Do not judge, or you too will be judged. ... Why do you look at the speck of sawdust in your brother's eye and pay no attention to the plank in your own eye? ... You hypocrite, first take the plank out of your own eye, and then you will see clearly to remove the speck from your brother's eye."

It is important to recognize when your personal issues may influence an encounter with another person. If you desire to help others explore options, then answer these questions honestly:

❑ Yes   ❑ No   Does the dilemma feel too close to you?

❑ Yes   ❑ No   Am I doing this so I feel needed?

❑ Yes   ❑ No   Am I helping this individual so I will feel important?

❑ Yes   ❑ No   Do I lose objectivity when listening to the other person's predicament?

If you answered yes to any of these questions, explore ways to resolve your own issues:
- for your emotional health
- for the benefit of others
- to serve God better and more joyfully

Reflect
- Which one or two personal issues that I am now aware of do I want to begin confronting in my own life?

- What will I begin doing to overcome these issues?

- Who can help me work through them?

Is Confrontation Needed?

It may become evident that the person's problem involves sin or other issues that need confronting. If so, confrontation may be necessary as an initial part of the solution-finding process. If inappropriate attitudes or behaviors are part of the problem, they must be addressed before the issue can be resolved.[2]

How Removed from Reality Is the Person?

When you are listening to someone's problem, often how you interpret what he tells you is actually three times removed from reality! He may have had something small happen, but he perceives it as bigger than it was. When he describes it to you, it gets bigger. Then how you interpret the situation, based on his description, can seem explosive. As a result, you

---

2 See the Appendix for more help on diagnosing people's problems.

may need to determine what the truth is about what he is saying. See the illustration below.

Reality → His Perception → His Description → Your Interpretation

Warning Signs You're Becoming Controlling

Before you can begin to assist others in solving their problems, you may need to determine if you have a tendency to be too controlling. If you do, it will diminish your effectiveness in helping them. There are many possible warning signs you are becoming bossy. Consider the following. Do you ever do or see these?

1. The person is crying and you are telling them what to do. If so, you probably haven't spent enough time listening or the person doesn't feel like you've heard him. You might need to go back and study Keys #2 and #3 in *Boost Your Relationship IQ.*

2. The person may be nodding his head, but doesn't seem to be engaged with the process. This should be all about the person you are helping, not about you and your need to fix people.

3. You are getting too emotionally involved in the scenario. You may need to take a step back and ask God why you are so involved. Also, consider how you can let go of your own needs, fears, wants or hurts so you can help someone else.

4. The person changes the subject when you try to help him resolve his issue. There might be other reasons for changing the subject, such as he hasn't had sufficient time to talk about the issue before you jumped into solving it. However, sometimes people will change the subject when they feel like solving this problem is more about you and your need to control than it is about them and their issue.

What other signs can you think of, based on what people have done or said to you?

Core Beliefs about Empowering Healthy Change

Your core beliefs determine how you live your life. Remember, a core belief is a firmly held conviction that consistently motivates your behavior.

Belief + Consistent Action = Core Belief

Core Belief #1

When I help people learn problem-solving skills,
I also help them grow in the Lord.

Think about this core belief and answer the following questions:

1. Do you believe it and live it in your relationships? Why or why not?

2. If not, what might you need to change to be effective in ministry?

3. What does this mean in your personal life? In your professional life?

4. How does helping someone learn problem-solving skills help him grow in the Lord?

5. What could you change in your core beliefs that might enrich your relationships with the following people?
   - your spouse

   - your children

   - friends

   - coworkers

   - people on your team, in your mission and in other communities

Core Belief #2

I don't always have to have the answers for other people's problems!

When someone has a problem, most people think they must have all the answers, especially if they are leaders. Is that you?

Having an answer is often dependent upon whether the issue is head level or heart level. For example, if you're a computer expert, it's appropriate for you to give answers to technical questions. Or you may need to discover the answer.

However, heart issues are different. People want someone to listen and give them an opportunity to explore and discover their own answers.

Think about Core Belief #2 and answer the following questions:

1. What does this mean to you in your personal life? In your communities— at home, ministry or church?

2. Do you live this core belief out? Why or why not?

3. What might you need to change about your core belief that could enrich your relationships with the following people?

   - your spouse

   - your children

   - friends

   - coworkers

   - people on your team, in your mission and in other communities

Core Belief #3

Giving advice may hurt others.

Think about Core Belief #3 and answer the following questions:

1. How could giving advice hurt a person?

2. Do you believe this core belief and act on it? Why or why not?

3. If you don't live this in your relationships, what might you need to change?

4. What could you change in the way you react to individuals who come to you with a problem?

Questions for Personal or Group Study

Consider the following alone or with a group:

1. Review this Key.

   a. What stands out for you?

b. Write down any areas in which you need to improve. What will you do to grow in each area?

2. Look at the illustration in Chapter 14, "Where Are You?" Find someone to practice with on responding on the right level.

   a. One person makes a statement.

   b. The second must determine what level the comment is on and respond appropriately.

   c. Discuss whether the response was helpful and what might have made it more useful.

   d. Trade roles.

   e. Practice several times with statements on both the heart level and the head level.

3. What personal qualities do you see in the following verses that will benefit you to help people solve problems?

   Psalm 37:30 (NIV): "The mouths of the righteous utter wisdom, and their tongues speak what is just."

   Psalm 111:10 (ESV): "The fear of the Lord is the beginning of wisdom; all those who practice it have a good understanding. His praise endures forever!"

   Proverbs 2:6 (NKJV): "The Lord gives wisdom; from his mouth come knowledge and understanding."

   Proverbs 11:2 (NLT): "Pride leads to disgrace, but with humility comes wisdom."

Proverbs 14:29 (NIV): "Whoever is patient has great understanding, but one who is quick-tempered displays folly."

Proverbs 16:23 (CJB): "The wise man's heart teaches his mouth, and to his lips it adds learning."

4. Consider any *personal issues* that may hinder you from being effective in helping others solve their problems. Consider topics such as these:

   a. A need to be needed

   b. A core belief that giving advice is the best way to help individuals solve their difficulties

   c. An unhealthy need to fix people's predicaments

   d. A fear of not having the answers people need

   e. An attitude that you know more than the other person

5. What do these verses say to you about giving advice?

    Proverbs 18:13 (NIV): "To answer before listening—that is folly and shame."

    Proverbs 18:2 (NLT): "Fools have no interest in understanding; they only want to air their own opinions."

6. Can you see any warning signs in yourself that you may be bossy or controlling? If so, what will you do about them? You might want to ask someone to hold you accountable.

7. Look at each of the core beliefs in this chapter.

    a. What did you learn from them?

    b. Are your core beliefs healthy or is there anything you might need to change based on what you learned? If so, what? How will you make those changes?

If you didn't work through each of the questions posed in this chapter, go back and answer them now. You might want to write your thoughts in a journal.

A Verse to Meditate On and Memorize

Choose a verse from this chapter. If you are not sure which to choose, try this one:

Proverbs 27:17 (NIV): "As iron sharpens iron, so one person sharpens another."

Snapshots

Go to the section titled "Snapshots" to record points you want to remember and/or do.

Chapter 18

A Prescription for Healthy Change

The mouths of the righteous utter wisdom, and their tongues speak what is just.
Psalm 37:30

Running a ministry and raising my sons, Jonathan and Timothy, on my own from the time they were four and ten was very difficult at times. During one particularly hard time, I needed to make a major decision about what to do with one of my sons. With no clear-cut answers, I began seeking solutions from friends and family members. Each person said something like,

"Have you tried ____?"

"Yes."

"Well, have you done ____?"

"Yep!"

"How about such and such?"

Every solution they came up with I had already tried. It would have been less frustrating for all of us if they had used the process I'm going to show you.

You can use the seven practical steps in this chapter with anyone to help them discover their own solutions. Thousands of people worldwide have proven the power in this skill. As I've taught missionary counselors, many who have PhDs, I've been amazed at how many of them never learned this powerful information to help their counselees. Some said this skill transformed their counseling practice. But you don't have to be a counselor to use this skill.

How Do I Help People Solve Their Problems?

A process called "exploring options" is an effective way to find solutions. It can be a catalyst to stimulate a person's creative thinking. This method provides a unique opportunity for ministry to believers and not-yet-believers. Consider the following:

- This procedure is a gift you give to other people after prayerfully asking for God's guidance.
- The goal of investigating choices involves encouraging the individual to consider all the possibilities to solve his dilemma.
- The ability to explore options with others is a vital skill, enabling you to help them discover *their own way* out of their problems.
- An active dependence on God as your source of wisdom is crucial in this process. Proverbs 16:1 (NIV) says, "To humans belong the plans of the heart, but from the Lord comes the proper answer of the tongue."
- This interactive process encourages creative thinking, opening minds to the Lord's direction and wisdom.
- Exploring options gives people with a problem an opportunity to carefully consider some of the many possibilities for solving it. The goal is to help them apply one or more options. The process is interactive and encourages creative thinking and opening their minds to the Lord's guidance and wisdom.

Proverbs 20:5 (ESV) says, "The purpose in a man's heart is like deep water, but a man of understanding will draw it out."

Why Explore Options?

At times all an individual wants is for you to listen, care and bear his burdens. However, a deeper need may be for practical real-life answers to problems. Authentic caring respects another person's freedom to make decisions with the potential to produce success or failure. If you respond by telling him what you think he should do, it is your solution, not his.

Supporting a person by helping him find his own answers takes longer than giving advice. However the results usually have greater effect. This process can do the following:

- Give solutions he is much more likely to implement because he discovered them on his own
- Build confidence as he pursues and discovers his own answers
- Provide the opportunity to carefully consider all of his alternatives and listen to the Holy Spirit
- Encourage him to work toward a more rewarding outcome
- Equip him with creative, problem-solving skills to resolve future quandaries; often people need *more* than just a way out of one predicament

Timing—The Key to Exploring Options

Timing is crucial. Have you ever heard the phrase "putting the cart before the horse"? Imagine trying to negotiate a cart down a road when your horse is pushing it, rather than pulling it. How effective do you think that would be?

It is important to make sure a person is ready to discover and explore his alternatives to resolve his dilemma. There is danger in moving to this step of exploring options too soon. He may still need to do the following:

- Process and think through his circumstances.
- Discuss his troubles on a heart level.
- Receive understanding, acceptance and encouragement—not judgment. If you begin this process too soon, he misses an opportunity to share his burdens and he isn't ministered to on a heart level. Galatians 6:2 (NIV) tells us, "Carry each other's burdens, and in this way you will fulfill the law of Christ."
- Sort out any cloudy thinking after talking freely in an accepting environment. Often a person cannot perceive his situation clearly until he has talked it out in a caring relationship. His thinking may be clouded and the fog may clear as he sorts it out by talking. Only then will he be able to see viable solutions.

We must sense when a person has been sufficiently ministered to on a heart level and is ready to go on to the head level to find solutions. Sensitivity to the right timing is extremely important. As you listen to him, he will begin to make that quiet transition from the need to share from the heart to the need to find solutions.

Sometimes the problem is on a head level and his emotions are not involved. In this situation, it is still important to listen well to enable the person to talk out the dilemma. This enables both of you to understand the problem and possible solutions better.

If the person asks for solutions before adequately talking about his predicament, encourage him to share more first.

- Listen quietly, so he can share his struggles in detail.
- Ask relevant questions. Key #4 in *Boost Your Relationship IQ* gives four types of questions and how to effectively use each one.
- Use self-disclosure and/or observations to draw him out (see Chapter 13 in *Boost Your Relationship IQ*). Then keep quiet so he will share.
- To encourage him to talk, say something like, "Tell me more about

the situation." This helps him to begin shifting from sharing from the heart to finding solutions. Of course, his need for empathy and caring will continue throughout this process.

Seven Steps to Opening the Door to Solutions

When you sense the timing is right, invite the person to explore ways to handle his problem. Walk through the process below with him. Note: this process does take some time, but it is worth it if you want to empower people for lifelong change. It can give them the motivation they need to solve their problems. It offers a powerful opportunity for people to learn a life-changing skill.

Go through each step below.

1. **Inquire, "What have you already tried?"** Then ask these questions for each solution he attempted:
    *   What happened when you tried that option?
    *   What difficulties did you experience?
    *   What were the positive outcomes?
    *   How did you feel about the experience?
    *   How does this affect your willingness to try again?

2. **Ask, "What have you thought about doing, but haven't tried?"**

    He may have already thought about several other options he has not tried. It is important to recognize these things:
    *   The total range of choices he has considered
    *   The reasons he hasn't tried the other possibilities
    *   How much he has pondered the situation
    *   How trapped he may feel
    *   What fears he may have in moving ahead with a solution

3. **Ask, "Can you think of any new options you haven't yet considered?"** Gently press him for new ideas. Don't dismiss any ideas at this stage. As he talks, he may begin to be aware of other possible solutions. This will help him to
    *   brainstorm creative ways to work through the concern;
    *   seek to expand his mind to creatively consider his situation;
    *   create new lines of thinking about the situation or solution;
    *   consider specific areas of the problem to attack.

4. **After you have thoroughly explored the first three steps, you can suggest other possibilities.**

- After satisfactorily completing steps 1 through 3, you may not need to offer your own solutions. If he has investigated many previous, untried and new options, you will not need to offer any of your own.
- If he runs out of ideas or none of his seem viable, you can recommend thoughts of your own for his consideration.

5 **Discover the pros and cons for each viable option.**

- Ask him to consider the positive and negative consequences of each choice he is seriously considering. Writing them down may help him see the bigger picture.
- Give feedback regarding his perception of reality.
- Recognize any tendency he may have to be too optimistic or pessimistic.
- Provide a balanced perspective.

6. **Assist him to pick one or more options and outline a step-by-step process to implement.**

- Based upon his pros and cons, help him choose and put into action his best options.
- Avoid pressuring him to make an immediate choice, unless it is urgently required by the demands of the situation.
- Make sure the decision is his choice, not yours. Even though he may see his options, he may need direction to apply them.
- If he is unwilling to take action, help him contemplate any feelings of reluctance or fear.
- Help him consider when and how he will start to implement his plan into action.

7. **Follow up with him.** Invite him to become accountable to you. Suggest he commit to applying at least one of the options. Set a specific time you will connect with him about this. It will give him motivation to apply the solution before you contact him.

When you contact him, ask:

- Which choice(s) did you try?
- What happened? Was the outcome positive or negative?
- Do you feel the problem is solved? If not, what is your next step?
- If it isn't resolved, you may need to go through these steps again.

Three Critical Skills to Empower Instead of Enable

Here are three skills that will help you empower others:

1. The ability to listen to the person and draw him out

2. A willingness to confront the person if he

   - seems like he would rather complain about the situation rather than trying to fix it
   - is sinning
   - doesn't follow through on the option he chose

3. The capacity to put aside your own ideas and all your "wonderful advice" and allow the person to figure out a solution himself (with your guidance, of course)

As you look at these skills, which might you need to work on? What will you do to improve in them?

What Happens If ...?

The following are possible challenges you may face as you try to help people solve their dilemmas. After each one, there are a few ideas to help you overcome the issues.

An option didn't work

- Identify what he did.
- Uncover the reasons his choice didn't work.
- Don't assume he followed through on the first try.
- Encourage him to try new alternatives or possibly retry the option again.

An option wasn't tried

- Why didn't he try it?
- If he makes excuses for not following through, gently explore if he wants a solution. Maybe his problem is providing more "payoff" than he realizes. For example, he may be more comfortable with his self-pity than being free from the dilemma.

Fears or procrastination prevented him from applying the options

- Help him look at what hinders him from taking action.
- Is his fear of confronting greater than his desire to solve the problem? If so, talk through possible ways to overcome his fear.
- Address why he procrastinates or fails to follow through.
- Brainstorm ways to overcome them in the future.

An option worked

- Assess what he learned from the experience.
- Identify how he can integrate this skill into his life. How can he apply the knowledge he gained to resolve future difficulties?
- Reinforce and affirm the successful principles he employed.
- Help him see any scriptural guidelines he employed or violated in the process.

Questions for Personal or Group Study

Consider the following alone or with a group:

1. Review this Key.

    a. What stands out for you?

    b. Write down any areas in which you need to improve. What will you do to grow in each area?

2. What do you think about "exploring options" when people come to you with problems? How do you think it could help them?

3. Think about a problem you have had or may currently have. Could you benefit from the "exploring options" process? Ask someone to work through it with you.

4. What can you learn about helping people solve problems from these Scriptures?

    Job 34:3–4 (NIV): "The ear tests words as the tongue tastes food. Let us discern for ourselves what is right; let us learn together what is good."

Proverbs 15:22 (NIV): "Plans fail for lack of counsel, but with many advisers they succeed."

5. Study the "Seven Steps to Opening the Door to Solutions."

   a. Memorize the steps so you will be ready to use them when opportunities arise.

   b. Which steps are most difficult for you? Why?

   c. What might you need to do to overcome any obstacles in using these steps?

6. Which, if any, of the challenges under "What Happens If ...?" have you experienced?

   a. How did you overcome them?

   b. If you didn't, consider what you could have done that might have worked.

A Verse to Meditate On and Memorize

Choose a verse from this chapter. If you are not sure which to choose, try this one:

Psalm 37:30 (NIV): "The mouths of the righteous utter wisdom, and their tongues speak what is just."

Snapshots

Go to the section titled "Snapshots" to record points you want to remember and/or do.

Chapter 19

How Can I Help Others with Their Problems?

Carry one another's burdens; in this way you will fulfill the law of Christ.
Galatians 6:2 HCSB

I remember many times when I went to my dad with a problem I needed to solve. After he listened and drew me out so he understood the issue, he would say, "What have you tried?" We would both laugh because we knew what he was doing. But then we walked through each of the steps in the last chapter. I can do them myself, but there is something powerful about exploring options with someone else. Many times as I talked with my dad, I would come up with a fabulous solution I had never thought about before!

Think about what a gift it can be to use this skill with those closest to you.

In this chapter you will do the following:
- Assess how you are doing at helping others solve their problems.
- Study real-life scenarios to see how you would normally react to them.
- Learn new ways to react.

These are not "tests" on which you will receive grades. Rather they are an opportunity for you to figure out areas that need work.

How Am I at Being a Catalyst for Change?

Consider how you are doing at helping others solve problems. Rate yourself with your family as well as other people. You could also include close friends or roommates if you don't live with your family. Use this scale to indicate your responses.

1 = Hardly ever; 2 = Occasionally; 3 = Sometimes;
4 = Often; 5 = Nearly always

Family Others

_____ _____ 1. When anyone talks about his problems, I don't have a need to provide all the answers.

_____ _____ 2. When an individual communicates on a heart level, I am willing to listen without trying to help solve his dilemma.

_____ _____ 3. I listen patiently when someone shares his difficulties. I don't begin trying to help him solve them until he clearly indicates he is ready.

_____ _____ 4. I avoid trying to get anyone to feel or think the way I believe he *should*.

_____ _____ 5. If I believe someone is engaging in gossip or slander rather than wanting help to solve his issue, I lovingly confront him.

_____ _____ 6. I try to discern whether others feel discouraged, hopeless, overconfident or overly optimistic about finding solutions to their difficulties.

_____ _____ 7. When a person is ready, I try to find out all of the ways he has tried to solve the problem and how he feels about what he tried.

_____ _____ 8. I explore with him all of the options he has considered to resolve the issue and what he thinks about each possibility.

_____ _____ 9. I try to help him break down the quandary into its different components. I encourage him to look at resolutions to each element.

_____ _____10. I give my advice or possible choices only after adequately exploring the previous three steps in numbers 7, 8 and 9 above.

_____ _____11. I avoid judging what he says he has done, has thought about doing or any other new possibilities he discovers.

_____ _____12. I help him explore the pros and cons of his options.

_____ _____13. When he decides to try an alternative, I help him be specific about what he will do, as well as when, where and how he will try each.

_____ _____14. I set up a time to check with him during the process and after he has finished trying his choice(s).

_____ _____15. Any need I have to fix other people's predicaments is under the control of the Holy Spirit.

_____ _____16. I pray for him while he attempts the solution.

Look over your responses to "How Am I at Being a Catalyst for Change?"

1. What difference did you see in how you respond to your family or close friends versus other people? Is there anything you may need to do differently in either category?

2. Congratulate yourself! Did you score a 4 or a 5 in any of the situations? You are doing great!

3. Needs Improvement. Did you score a 3? Once you have improved the 1s and 2s, work on the 3s.

4. If you scored a 1 or 2:

   a. Write out an action plan to improve each area of concern.

    b. Choose one or two elements of your action plan to begin working on right now. Which will you start with?

5. Talk with someone you trust who will hold you accountable.

    a. Who will you talk to?

    b. When will you call (time and date)?

Hypothetical Scenarios

Look at each of these real-life stories. Then answer the questions following them.

Your Friend's Father Wants Her to Move in with Him. A year ago, Grace's husband of ten years was suddenly killed in an auto accident. Only thirty-two years old, she decided to stay with your mission and continue serving God in the home office. Relying on the Lord, Grace is beginning to regain her self-confidence as an independent woman and mother of young children. After her mother died recently, her father, who lives in another state, began to insist she move in with him to help him. Grace does not want to move, but he is pressuring her. She longs to figure out the best options for both her family and her father.

1. How would you normally respond to this situation?

2. What have you learned from this Key that could help you respond better?

3. Review "Seven Steps to Opening the Door to Solutions" in Chapter 18. How could you implement these principles in this situation?

4. What might you need to do to prepare yourself to handle a situation like this?

5. How do you think applying these steps might help Grace grow stronger personally and spiritually?

6. Which step would be the most difficult for you in this situation?

Your Friend Is in Debt and Can't Pay His Bills. Jason has been your best friend since you were in Bible college together. You became a missionary; he went into business. At his last pool party, you marveled that he lives in a mansion, wears designer label clothing and drives a large expensive car. You are surprised when you receive his desperate phone call, confessing he is in heavy debt. He cannot afford his house payments, gardener, pool maintenance and credit card bills. Not only does he not have enough money for the payments on his car, he can barely pay for gas. Jason can no longer hold off his creditors and he is not sure what to do. He hints you should loan him money to tide him over, which is not an option because your support is very low. How can you help Jason solve his problems?

1. How would you normally respond to this situation?

2. What have you learned from this Key that could help you respond better?

3. How could you implement what you learned in this Key to this situation?

4. What might you need to do to prepare yourself to handle something like this?

5. How do you think going through this process might help Jason grow stronger personally and spiritually?

6. Which step would be the most difficult for you in this situation?

Questions for Personal or Group Study

Consider the following alone or with a group:

1. Review this Key.

    a. What stands out for you?

b. Write down any areas in which you need to improve. What will you do to grow in each area?

2. What can you learn about helping people solve problems from the Scriptures below?

Proverbs 20:18 (ESV): "Plans are established by counsel; by wise guidance wage war."

Proverbs 27:17 (NIV): "As iron sharpens iron, so one person sharpens another."

Proverbs 29:20 (NKJV): "Do you see a man hasty in his words? There is more hope for a fool than for him."

3. What did you learn from the self-assessment? What areas do you most need to work on?

4. As you went through each of the scenarios, what stood out to you?

a. What might you need to work on before you can most effectively use the skill in this Key?

   b. If you are in a group, discuss some of the questions in each scenario. What can you learn from each other?

5. What might you need to do to become more aware of these things?

   a. How you give advice

   b. When you present your opinion

   c. To whom you offer suggestions

6. At the end of conversations stop and ask yourself if you gave advice when

   a. Listening might have had greater benefits

   b. It might have been more helpful for the person to explore his options

Pray for each other and yourself as you learn this skill, which is probably new to most of you.

A Verse to Meditate On and Memorize

Choose a verse from this chapter. If you are not sure which to choose, try this one:

   Galatians 6:2 (HCSB): "Carry one another's burdens; in this way you will fulfill the law of Christ."

Snapshots

Go to the section titled "Snapshots" to record points you want to remember and/or do.

Chapter 20

How Can I Empower Others to Solve Their Problems?

Who is wise and understanding among you?
Let them show it by their good life,
by deeds done in the humility that comes from wisdom.
James 3:13 NIV

Learning any new skill takes practice and time. When I went to Guatemala as a missionary, first I had to learn Spanish, getting up to a high proficiency level. Once that was completed I could move to the village of Yepocapa to learn the unwritten Kaqchikel language. (They didn't even have an alphabet—that would be part of our job.)

Learning Spanish took many months. I studied language-learning principles with a class. Then we created routes that we individually took every day. We found people in stores who were willing to let us practice our Spanish with them. Daily we learned new phrases and then went to each of the locations on our routes to practice what we were learning.

Just as we couldn't expect to immediately be proficient in Spanish, neither can you expect to be immediately proficient in learning new interpersonal skills. They take practice. Once we learned the language, it was easy to converse with people, without having to think through each word, sentence, inflection and so on. In the same way, as you practice this skill, you will find it becoming easier.

I encourage you to take the time to practice this skill until it becomes natural and you can use it without having to consider each step. Practice makes perfect in any skill; however, you need to make sure you are practicing the skill correctly.

Overview

Here is an overview of what you'll do in this chapter:

1. Watch a video demonstrating the skill and write what you discover.

2. Discuss what you learned in the demonstration.

3. Practice this skill with a partner.

4. Debrief what you learned and how you can apply it in your life.

Demonstration on Empowering Others to Solve Problems

If you are working through this course alone, find someone to go through this chapter with you. It is impossible to practice this skill by yourself.

Watch the video demonstrating how to apply the seven steps to a problem. Notice how each step was handled. Assume there has already been sufficient listening to the problem and how it affects the person. The purpose of this demonstration is to show the seven steps rather than to reveal how to listen.[1]

As you watch the video, write down what you observe. How do you see the man in the video use each of these skills?

1. Asking what she already tried

2. Asking what she thought of but hasn't tried

3. Inviting her to think of new options

4. Suggesting ideas of his own

5. Exploring pros and cons of any viable ideas

6. Helping choose and apply options

7. Following up

Debrief

Talk with your partner about the following questions:

1. What did you learn as you watched the video?

2. How were each of the steps applied?

---

1 You can learn how to listen and draw the person out in the book or online course, *Boost Your Relationship IQ*. Learn more at www.RelationshipResources.org.

3. What might be difficult for you in using this process?

Practice Helping Others Solve Their Problems

Now it is time for you to practice this critical skill.

To practice, do the following:

1. Decide which of you will be the first to practice the skill and which will have the *problem* to address.

2. Look at the "Issues to Use for Practice" below. Choose one to practice.

3. Go through the "Seven Steps to Opening the Door to Solutions" in Chapter 18. Keep it in front of you to remind you of other questions you can ask. It gives you detailed questions on each step so you can thoroughly help the person.

4. Be sure to keep asking for options in each step until the person runs out of alternatives.

5. During your practice, skip step #4 (suggesting other possibilities) because that one comes naturally for most people.

6. Switch roles so you both have a chance to practice the skill. You can use the same problem or a different one.

7. As you practice, avoid getting caught up in the issue addressed. Rather, focus on the skill.

8. Make sure you go through each of the steps in order.

9. If you have a video camera or voice recorder, record your practice sessions, then review what you can do better. Write what you discover for each step.

Issues to Use for Practice

Choose one of the following issues to practice. Make sure any scenario you use has several possible solutions so the process will work.

1. Choose a real dilemma you have had in the past, you have now or someone you know has had.

2. A friend has a relative who was offended and hardly speaks to him.

3. Someone from your mission team just received lab results. The diagnosis is terrifying and there is no clear option.

4. A coworker is not coping well with stress. He considers quitting his job.

5. Choose one of the hypothetical scenarios from Chapter 19.

Steps to Practice

Write the answers to each question. You will need this information for the latter steps.

1. Inquire, "What have you already tried?"

2. Ask, "What have you thought about doing, but haven't tried?"

3. Ask, "Can you think of any new options you haven't yet considered?"

4. (Skip this step in your practice, because suggesting options comes naturally for most people.)

5. Discover the pros and cons for each viable option.

6. Assist him to outline a step-by-step process to implement one or more options.

7. Follow up with him.

After you practice, talk about how it went:

1. What did you learn from the experience?

2. What problems did you experience?

3. What do you need to do differently in real life?

How to Stimulate Positive Change

Here are three strategies you can use to stimulate people to implement the positive changes they want to embrace:

1. Make sure *they* decide which option to use, not you. If they feel like it is your solution, they will not be as likely to follow through.

2. Ask for permission to follow up with them. Let them know you will be calling them to see how the solution worked and what, if anything, may need to be done differently.

3. Pray with and for the people before they leave, asking God to give them wisdom to implement His plan for their situations.

Questions for Personal or Group Study

Consider the following alone or with a group:

1. Review this Key.

   a. What stands out for you?

   b. Write down any areas in which you need to improve. What will you do to grow in each area?

2. How did your practice time go?

   a. What were your greatest challenges with doing it?

   b. How did it feel to be on the receiving end?

3. What personal qualities do you see in the following verses that will benefit you as you help people solve problems?

   1 Corinthians 13:4 (NIV): "Love is patient, love is kind. It does not envy, it does not boast, it is not proud."

   2 Corinthians 6:6 (CEV): "We have kept ourselves pure and have been understanding, patient, and kind. The Holy Spirit has been with us, and our love has been real."

   Ephesians 4:2 (NLT): "Always be humble and gentle. Be patient with each other, making allowance for each other's faults because of your love."

   Philippians 2:3 (ESV): "Do nothing from selfish ambition or conceit, but in humility count others more significant than yourselves."

   James 3:13 (NIV): "Who is wise and understanding among you? Let them show it by their good life, by deeds done in the humility that comes from wisdom."

4   Think about any times people have shared heart-level problems with you. How have you responded in the past?

5. When people share a heart-level problem with you, use the conversation as an opportunity to explore options with them, if they want to find solutions.

    a. After the conversation, note how many of the steps you used.

    b. Did you give the person advice?

    c. What was the outcome?

    d. What could you do differently next time?

6. If you have children, or you are in any leadership position, be aware of opportunities to explore options with them rather than giving advice. This applies to anyone over three years old!

7. Here are questions you might ask people who are close to you:

    a. How do you feel about the way I respond to you when you have a crisis?

    b. What do you think about the way I give you advice?

    c. How would you like me to respond when you have a problem?

To gain greater skills in exploring options, consider practicing with your spouse or a close friend. Use a real situation or a hypothetical one.

A Verse to Meditate On and Memorize

Choose a verse from this chapter. If you are not sure which to choose, you can use one of these. Spend time with the Lord and consider how the verse may apply to you:

Proverbs 18:13 (ESV): "If one gives an answer before he hears, it is his folly and shame."

James 3:13 (NIV): "Who is wise and understanding among you? Let them show it by their good life, by deeds done in the humility that comes from wisdom."

Snapshots

Go to the section titled "Snapshots" to record points you want to remember and/or do.

Strategy for Success

Review this Key.

1. What will you take away from it?

2. Write a brief account of a past or present situation.

3. Prayerfully consider which principles in this Key could be a catalyst for a positive outcome.

As you become skilled in helping others solve problems, you will experience growing joy in being used by God in people's lives.

Key #6: Overcome Obstacles

I will work hard to make sure you always
remember these things after I am gone.
2 Peter 1:15 NLT

When I, and probably you, first learned to drive a car, all the steps were overwhelming. I had to remember so many different processes: put on my seatbelt; make sure the car was in park; check the mirrors to make sure no one was close to me; turn on the car. Well ... you get the idea. After continually reviewing and practicing the skills for driving a car, eventually it became natural. However, the process took time and I had to overcome some obstacles to become a safe driver.

As I learned the skills in this book and put them into practice, I needed to review them and continue to practice them until they became part of me. Otherwise it would have been easy to get busy with other, "more important" duties and forget them. If we don't continue to apply the skills, we forget them and our relationships suffer.

Numerous times in the Old Testament, God told the people to remember Him and what He revealed to them. This Key is very important because it reminds us of what we've learned, so we can apply the principles and skills to our lives.

I challenge you to study this Key with an open mind, asking God what He wants you to remember and continue to grow in.

Chapter 21

What Now?

Let what I'm saying sink deeply into your hearts and souls.
Do whatever it takes to remember what I'm telling you.
Deuteronomy 11:18 VOICE

Now you have studied the principles and skills in this course, consider if you have any conflicts from the past you may need to revisit. Here are possible examples:

- Was there a time you responded poorly to a conflict and it hurt your relationship with that person? Ask the Lord, what you may need to do to repair that relationship?

- Who have you confronted poorly, resulting in damage to your relationship? If so, ask the Lord, what you may need to do to repair that relationship?

- Who has had a conflict with someone else, but you ignored it because you didn't know how to help them? If they are still in conflict, could you offer to help them now?

- Who has a solvable problem, but you were afraid to help him find a solution? Ask the Lord if you should call him now to see if he still wants help with his problem.

You've studied and applied the biblical skills in this book. Now what? Reviewing and continuing to apply the skills you've learned is imperative to see changes in your life and your community.

This chapter is to help you integrate the knowledge and skills gained in the book, so you can apply them more effectively. Working through these pages may be the most difficult part of the book for you, but it may also be the most helpful. Please thoughtfully respond to each question, using a separate sheet or journal, if necessary.

This is an opportunity to do a personal "audit" on how you are doing living in community. Look over the issues below. Ask God if there are any which you need to work on.

Commitments

As you go through this chapter, ask yourself these questions:

1. What commitments do I want to make to the Lord in these areas?

2. With whom will I be accountable for these commitments?

3. What Scriptures will I begin to memorize in order to do battle in my areas of concern?

Assessing My Response to This Book

Consider the material and skills presented and how you personally responded to them. Look over each chapter, including the "Snapshots" page to remind you of specific topics. Answer each question honestly.

1. Facts Presented

   a. Which topics gave me with the most helpful information and insights?

   b. As I think back over these topics, three or four specific ideas or insights which were new to me are:

c. The most important thing the Lord has spoken to me about this study is:

2. Skills Gained

a. Which skills especially stand out as being important to me personally as I minister to others?

b. Which skills are most important for the communities I'm a part of?

c. Of these skills, the one I need most in my life and ministry is:

d. The new skill I got the best handle on through this study is:

3. Application

a. Write one or more ways to apply insights from this study in relationships, such as, "Now that I realize listening is more important than advice, I plan to be more attentive when others are hurting and withhold unsolicited advice."

b. One specific way I can apply a new skill gained through this study to my relationships is:

c. One specific way I can apply a skill from this study that will improve my communities:

4. Most Impacting Scripture(s)

    a. Which verse or verses most impacted your life from this study?

    b. What verses did you memorize? Are there any you would like to memorize?

    c. What is one surprising truth from the Bible that you found? For example, we are commanded to encourage one another daily. It is not a suggestion or something to do when we *feel like* doing it. We are to do it every day.

Personal Examination

In this section you will look at your personal issues. As you consider insights gained or confirmed about yourself, prayerfully answer these questions.

1. My Core Beliefs

    a. Which of my core beliefs about conflict have been strengthened from this course?

    b. Which core beliefs have been dropped or updated?

    c. What new core beliefs am I beginning to hold as a result of this course?

2. My Needs and Fears

    a. What needs and/or fears am I now aware of that have been hindering me?

b. Which one(s) do I believe the Lord wants me to begin dealing with?

3. Application

Write *one goal* on how to begin to work on one core belief, need or fear. Specifically state the plan to do and when. For example, "I will share my need of _____ with my spouse/friend/pastor and ask him to remind me when it is hindering my relationships with him or others. I will begin praying daily that the Lord will empower me to overcome it."

Future Growth

Consider some specific ways in which you are committed to growing in the months ahead, based on your experience with this book.

1. Identifying and Overcoming Hindrances

a. What are two or three internal factors (weakness or other characteristics) which hinder my ability to handle conflict in ways that glorify God? For example, "difficulty concentrating, tendency to be judgmental, impatience, self-centeredness rather than other-centeredness."

b. What are two or three behavior patterns that hinder my ability to effectively manage conflict? For example, "a tendency to talk rather than listen and a habit of interrupting; I'm too quick to give advice."

c. Choose one internal factor or one behavior pattern to describe what can be done now to begin overcoming it. What will I do and when?

2. Commitment to Grow in Knowledge and/or Skills

    a. Write one goal to continue growing in knowledge and/or skills related to effectively manage conflict. For example, "set aside two hours a week to study through this book with my spouse," or "consciously apply _____ skills with people in my community for a month." (Specify with whom you will apply the skills.)

    b. A specific skill I will begin applying in my relationship with the following people:

    Person #1, skill to apply:

    Person #2, skill to apply:

    c. Get together with your spouse or someone else who studied this book to discuss issues, practice skills and pray together about growth in ministering to others.

    Whom would I like to approach for this purpose?

    When will I do it?

How to Improve Our Community

These are questions to discuss with your community. If you are in a large group, you might want to divide into groups of four to six people so everyone feels free to give their input. Then come together as a whole group and have a representative from each group share some of what their group discussed.

1. Each person should go through all the questions above.
2. Discuss how you can bring more glory to God through your community. What might you need to change?

3. What is keeping visitors from returning? What might you need to change?

4. What are you doing now to attract people? What else could you do?

5. How can you empower your whole community to live in ways that glorify God?

6. Revise, if necessary, "A Sample Covenant for Mission Communities" to meet your group's needs. Then have everyone sign it. It is on the next page.

7. Pray together asking God to reveal more to you.

Questions for Personal or Group Study

Rather than giving you more questions to consider, go through each of the questions in this chapter alone or with others. There is great power in sharing your answers with others. You can learn from each other and hold one another accountable to follow through on what you've decided.

May God richly bless you, and others whom you relate to, as you seek to apply what you learned in this book. I would love to hear how you've grown through your study. Feel free to email me at Gaylyn@ RelationshipResources.org.

A Sample Covenant for Mission Communities

Here is a sample covenant you can use with your mission or team. Talk through it and modify it to fit your group. Then encourage each person to sign it.

As God's children, relying on His life within us, we _____
_____, in light of our shared vision to serve God and our desire to glorify Him, commit ourselves to

- Love one another.
- Accept one another as Christ accepts us.
- Seek to build one another up in Christ.
- Care for one another's practical needs.
- Be vulnerable with one another, expressing our true needs and doubts, knowing that prayer and acceptance will accompany us.
- Graciously speak the truth to one another and hear the truth from one another in a spirit of love.
- Avoid gossip and slander and to keep one another from doing so.
- Keep short accounts with one another, being quick to forgive, so that grudges won't develop.
- Bear with one another when we find ourselves being impatient.
- Refuse to compare ourselves with each other.
- Seek the highest degree of consensus possible on major decisions.
- Work together in spite of differences of opinion and expectations, while having freedom to discuss them.
- Make an effort to understand and respect differing points of view.
- Avoid judging each other.
- Seek the Lord's direction together in prayer when we disagree.
- Be accountable to one another to fulfill this covenant.

Signed this _____ day of _____

_____
Signature

Appendices

About Us

The publisher, Relationship Resources

- Facilitates growth for believers and not-yet-believers in their relationships with God, themselves and other people.
- Provides practical, biblical, interactive workshops and materials designed to empower and equip individuals and groups in their lives, work and ministries.
- Trains and mentors facilitators to provide workshops for other groups.
- Gained IRS nonprofit status in 1999.
- Began as a concept in 1970 with Ken Williams' training missionaries
- Equips people to apply biblical principles to their relationships.
- Offers workshops on many topics, including:
  - o Boost Your Relationship IQ;
  - o Never Fear Conflict Again;
  - o Never Do Fundraising Again;
  - o Intimacy with God;
  - o Understanding Your Identity in Christ;
  - o Surprised by Joy;
  - o Stress Busters for Missionaries.

The author, Gaylyn Williams is

- The director of Relationship Resources, Inc. since 1999;
- Passionate about empowering people for maximum success in their lives and relationships;
- A published author of thirty-three books and four online courses;
- A magazine writer with numerous published articles in various magazines;
- An international motivational speaker and seminar trainer;
- Mother of two married sons, one grandson and one grand dog;

- A former missionary with Wycliffe Bible Translators from 1972 to 1992;
- A former missionary with The Navigators from 1997–1999.

Gaylyn inspires people to be all they can be spiritually, personally and relationally. She is a transparent and engaging author and speaker who creates an intimate rapport with her audience. Her insights are poignant and powerful as she encourages people in every area of their lives.

Having experienced heartbreaking losses as a child on the mission field and later as a woman and mother, Gaylyn's stories and illustrations beautifully reflect the power of God's sustaining grace.

Today she is passionate about equipping and encouraging people toward rediscovering joy, experiencing God's love, de-stressing their lives, building strong relationships, turning conflict into intimacy, and embracing new perspectives for a transformed life. Gaylyn offers practical, biblical insights that make a difference in lives and relationships.

Gaylyn has spoken to hundreds of organizations nationally and internationally, and has been featured on dozens of radio and television programs. She lives in view of the majestic Pikes Peak in Colorado Springs, Colorado.

What Gaylyn's listeners and readers are saying:

Is it really possible to live in joy when your life has been riddled with unthinkable pain? I am awed by a person who has mastered the task. Gaylyn shares a litany of life events that would have sent Goliath spiraling. Much like David the shepherd boy, she faced off with her giant and moved from defeat to victory! Her story held me captive—the unabridged truth came with force and clarity. It was clear she had spent time in the soul's abyss and came out a shining star. She is amazingly authentic.

Kimberly Faye, Author and Speaker

Gaylyn Williams and her incredible life story and spirit inspire all those who are fortunate enough to hear her speak or read her story. Gaylyn's humble, but powerful, style is laced with humor, grace, heartache, and joy, while her story embodies adventure, courage, triumph, and tragedy. By creatively sharing the lessons she learned along the way, Gaylyn helps the rest of us see how we too can apply those lessons to ease our own burdens.

Kris Harty, Author, Speaker and Stickabilities Specialist
www.StrongSpiritUnlimited.com

"Gaylyn, you are a very gifted and very special person. You are sharp, intelligent, in many ways strong and courageous, yet quiet, genuine, humble and a person with a lot of depth. For reasons known only to the Lord, He has led you through very deep waters. In the process He has formed you into the beautiful person that you are today. Your commitment to the Lord and His service is exemplary. He has given you a ministry that is impacting the world through the missionaries that you help. I'm sure that the only way you can go on is by the Lord's moment by moment pouring His strength, wisdom and grace into your mind, heart, emotions and body."

—*George Warren, Evangelical Free Church Mission*

Ken Williams, Ph.D

- He and his wife Bobbie began their ministry with Wycliffe Bible Translators in 1957. They first served among the Chuj people of Guatemala, completing a translation of the New Testament, as well as founding a Bible Institute, literacy work, and medical clinics.
- In the early 1970s Ken began providing care and counseling for cross-cultural workers. Ken earned his Ph.D. in Human Behavior, and he and Bobbie continued in this ministry with Wycliffe for twenty-two years, counseling thousands of missionaries worldwide.
- Ken came to realize that many of the difficult issues addressed in counseling could be avoided if believers received effective training in interpersonal relationships and managing stress. This was accompanied by Ken's deep conviction that healthy, godly relationships are best built and sustained by living out God's Word.
- In 1987 Ken began to develop training programs for workers in Christian ministries, especially mission organizations.
- In 1992 he began a ministry devoted to providing five-day intensive workshops in interpersonal skills. In 1999 he co-founded Relationship Resources and in 2001 he founded International Training Partners, Inc.
- Ken went home to be with Jesus in April 2013.

To learn more about us, go to www.RelationshipResources.org.

Scriptures about When the Issue May Be More Important Than the Relationship

The relationship is almost always more important than the issue. However, Scripture teaches us that in some cases our relationship with others must take second place to the issue. We need to know when to put the issue first, even if it means the relationship is harmed or broken. Here are examples:

Proverbs 5:8 (NIV): "Keep to a path far from her [an immoral person], do not go near the door of her house."

Proverbs 13:20 (NIV): "Walk with the wise and become wise, for a companion of fools suffers harm."

Proverbs 22:24–25 (NIV): "Do not make friends with a hot-tempered person, do not associate with one easily angered, or you may learn their ways and get yourself ensnared."

Titus 3:10 (NIV): "Warn a divisive person once, and then warn them a second time. After that, have nothing to do with them."

2 Thessalonians 3:6 (NIV): "In the name of the Lord Jesus Christ, we command you, brothers and sisters, to keep away from every believer who is idle and does not live according to the teaching you received from us."

2 Thessalonians 3:14–15 (ESV): "If anyone does not obey what we say in this letter, take note of that person, and have nothing to do with him, that he may be ashamed. Do not regard him as an enemy, but warn him as a brother."

2 Timothy 3:1–5 (ESV): "Understand this, that in the last days there will come times of difficulty. For people will be lovers of self, lovers of money, proud, arrogant, abusive, disobedient to their parents, ungrateful, unholy, heartless, unappeasable, slanderous, without self-control, brutal, not loving good, treacherous, reckless, swollen with conceit, lovers of pleasure rather than lovers of God, having the appearance of godliness, but denying its power. Avoid such people."

2 Timothy 4:14–15 (NKJV): "Alexander the coppersmith did me much harm. May the Lord repay him according to his works. You also must beware of him, for he has greatly resisted our words."

Titus 1:10–11 (NLT): "There are many rebellious people who engage in useless talk and deceive others. This is especially true of those who insist on circumcision for salvation. They must be silenced, because they are turning whole families away from the truth by their false teaching. And they do it only for money."

2 Peter 3:17 (NIV): "Dear friends, since you have been forewarned, be on your guard so that you may not be carried away by the error of the lawless and fall from your secure position."

2 John 1:9–10 (NIV): "Anyone who runs ahead and does not continue in the teaching of Christ does not have God; whoever continues in the teaching has both the Father and the Son. If anyone comes to you and does not bring this teaching, do not take them into your house or welcome them."

Diagnosing Problems

This discussion is not to be exhaustive, but covers a few principles of diagnosing problems for lay people, along with some common dangers. When a serious physical or emotional problem is suspected, be sure to urge the person to seek professional help.

Spiritual Resources Are Important in Diagnosis:

1. Only God knows the heart (Jeremiah 17:10; 1 Samuel 16:7).

2. His Word is effective for diagnosis (Hebrews 4:12–13).

3. He gives wisdom to those who ask (James 1:5).

4. He promises wisdom, insight, knowledge and understanding to those who seek it (Proverbs 2:1–6).

Issues to Consider in Diagnosing Problems

1. **Functioning**. As you interact with someone who is struggling, ask yourself if he able to function effectively in these areas:
   - personal life
   - close relationships with others
   - relationship with God
   - work or study responsibilities
   - social life

   If not, to what degree is he hindered now in each area? What differences are there between *his description* of his functioning and others' descriptions? Ask him how things are going in each area. If he speaks in generalities, ask for specifics.

2. **Pain**. How much is he hurting inside? Some people function quite well even when in deep emotional pain. Pain may be expressed verbally and nonverbally.

   In what specific ways is he hurting? Is he experiencing depression, anxiety, fear, guilt (real or false), unresolved grief, low self-esteem, self-hate, discouragement, inability to cope or alienation from others?

   If he doesn't specifically talk about his pain, rather than asking direct questions, invite him to talk by using tentative statements, such as, "It sounds like you're hurting."

3. **Difficulties in Perception.** To what degree and in what ways is his perception of reality hindered? How does he see himself, God, others, his close relationships, his present situation, work, his past, present and future and so on?

    - Invite him to discuss his perceptions. For example, "How do you see yourself? Your situation? Your marriage? Your work?"
    - Does he respond to reality in accord with his stated perceptions?
    - Does he consistently see *everything* as negative or positive?
    - How congruent is he in his speech and nonverbal communication? For example, does he describe a terrible situation with a smile?
    - Does he perceive his situation as hopeless? Be careful that you don't get caught up in his distortion of reality.

4. **Factors Influencing His Condition.** No problem happens in a vacuum. Try to discern what issues are underlying the problem.

    - *What predisposing factors appear to be affecting him?* For example, genetic tendencies, childhood abuse or long-term negative attitudes.
    - *What precipitating factors are affecting him?* For example, stressors, family problems or physical illness.

5. Trends. What trends have there been in his problem areas?

    - Has he been getting better, worse or staying the same?
    - At what rate has change been happening?
    - Is this a chronic or acute problem?
    - Is he stable? If not, is he deteriorating rapidly or slowly?

    If he doesn't discuss trends, ask, "How are things now compared to last week? Last month? Last year?" You might ask him to draw a graph of his condition over the past few weeks, months or years.

6. **Coping Ability.**

    - How able is he to apply resources in resolving his difficulties?
    - How well is he coping now?
    - What kinds of things are hindering his ability to cope?
    - In what ways can you help him in this?

Six Common Dangers to Avoid in Diagnosis

1. **Assuming that the first problem is the real problem.** He may not know what the real problem is or he may bring up a less threatening issue to test how you will react.

2. **Confusing symptoms with root problems.** What he believes is the root problem may only be a symptom, which may be unrelated or remotely related. Often the pain itself is seen as the problem.

3. **Making firmly held hypotheses too quickly.** You will probably begin to make hypotheses right away, often unconsciously. These can hinder or help. Be aware of them and hold on to them loosely. Do not verbalize them too quickly; they can lead you astray.

4. **Oversimplifying**.
   - *Oversimplifying the causes.* For example, saying, "It's a spiritual problem." There are often multiple causes, which may not be the obvious surface causes.
   - *Oversimplifying the solutions.* What may seem to be an obvious solution to you may be irrelevant. What worked for you or someone else may not work at all for him.

5. **Judging or condemning.** See Romans 2:1–3; 8:31–34. Judging can severely hinder your perception and ability to diagnose accurately. It will also cut off open communication.

6. **Assuming that what you hear is reality.** It's actually three times removed from reality as we saw in Chapter 17!

You may not be able to solve every person's problem, but you can be of great help by understanding how serious it may be. Then you are able to encourage him to get whatever help he needs.

Four Stages of Building New Patterns

This book challenges you to examine how well you communicate. The core beliefs provide a new way of thinking to enrich your life based on God's Word, in order to build and rebuild successful relationships.

Like remodeling a house, the step-by-step learning process helps you identify the actions you need to incorporate to be more effective in all areas of your life. As you complete the activities, you develop your communication abilities and increase your understanding of Scripture. Below are the stages to learning a new skill.

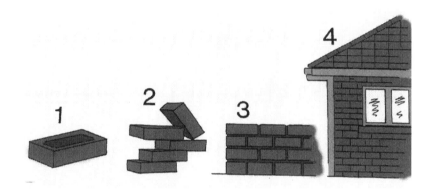

Stage 1   Awareness Stage: You become aware of a new skill.

Stage 2   Awkward Stage: At first it feels awkward and unnatural as you start practicing it. You may become stuck at this stage and give up.

Stage 3   Do it by the numbers: The ability no longer feels awkward, but you still have to deliberately concentrate on how to perform; otherwise, you fall back into old patterns.

Stage 4   Integration: You find yourself performing the skill automatically; it becomes a part of you.

Leader's Guide for Small Groups

You can use these suggestions for any small groups, including with your spouse and/or children.

Leading a group discussion is a rewarding experience. It can also be frightening, especially if it's your first time. By giving specific suggestions, this guide will help facilitate group discussion. As you prepare and lead the group, remember 2 Corinthians 12:9: "My grace is sufficient for you, for my power is made perfect in weakness." Accept His grace and power to lead your group.

Here are some ideas that may help you:

1. Pray that God will give wisdom and guidance as you study to learn everything He wants to teach you personally, as well as to effectively lead the discussion. Also pray for God to give all group members understanding and excitement as they study.
2. Start and end on time. Begin each class with prayer.
3. Before each session, choose between one and ten pages to study. You might want to discuss with your group how many pages they want to study for the week.
4. Have each person look up study and meditate on the truths on the pages you will study. It is more important to go deeper in the study than to get through more truths. Each person should use a separate notebook to write down what the Lord is showing them through each truth about how God sees them.
5. In the first session, as well as whenever anyone new begins the class, tell everyone that everything shared in the study is completely confidential. Get an agreement from participants that they will not share outside the group, anything they hear in the group–including talking to each other about another member, when they are not present.
6. Encourage each member to participate but be sensitive to the shy ones. Never call on anyone who has not volunteered to share. Wait until they are ready to talk, otherwise the group may feel unsafe to those who are more introverted.
7. During the session, ask the following questions and allow the group to discuss each one:
8. Which truths of how God sees you stood out to you and why?
9. Which verses ministered to you and why?
10. What is the Lord teaching you as you get to know how He sees you?

End each class with a time of prayer, giving participants an opportunity to share with God whatever is on their heart.

In the first session, if the group members don't know each other, have everyone briefly introduce themselves. Keep it short so you have time for the Bible Study.

Enjoy your study. As you share with your group, you will learn even more than you would on your own.

Facilitator Training

Would you like to lead groups where people are eager to return? Would you like to transform people's lives through training? You can do both if you learn a few simple principles.

Relationship Resources trains people to effectively facilitate groups, using our materials and adult learning principles. Participants will acquire the tools needed for leading our workshops or using their material to facilitate any training or workshop.

Learn How to Lead Small Groups

We offer practical principles and intensive experiential training, where participants practice how to effectively lead groups. In this course you will learn to use the following:

- Large group interaction
- Small group interaction
- Skill demonstrations and practice
- Reflection and self-assessments

Most if not all of us teach and train others because we sincerely want to make a difference in people's lives. We want to help people grow in their relationship with God, others and in their practical skills for life. Do you know how to accomplish that?

Adult Learning

Our Christian culture teaches us that adults learn through lecture or sermons. Our culture says that the more information we can cram down people's throats, the more they will learn. Consequently we try to shove as much of our knowledge into others in as short a time as possible. Yet statistics show that the opposite is true.

In these classes, we look at some of these statistics that reveal that lecture and monologues are not ideal, if we want to make a difference in people's lives. We need to get people involved in their own learning.

We discuss and practice these and many other axioms of adult learning:

- Take advantage of the teachable moment
- Trust your intuition
- Don't tell what you can ask; don't ask if you know the answer; tell, in dialogue

- Don't decide for learners what they can decide for themselves
- Design training to evoke the energy that is in the group
- None of us is as smart as all of us
- Adults learn by doing

Contact Us

Contact us if you would like us to offer a workshop for your community or you would like to find out about being trained to facilitate workshops using our materials.

Comfort Zones

Your living, work, social and communication experiences comprise your comfort zone. This mental boundary makes you feel secure and safe rather than anxious or threatened. However, these internal limits may result in limited personal, relational and spiritual growth as a Christian.

Your comfort zone directly affects your hopes and dreams as well as your personal, family and professional relationships. You may need to do the following:

- Identify what you are currently doing that *is* and *is not* working in how you relate to others.
- Learn new skills to develop in areas that are not functioning properly. Once the new abilities are automatic, your old comfort zone will be unacceptable to you.

The core beliefs in this book will help you move forward in ways that benefit your spiritual development.

There are two basic types of comfort zones.

Small, Carefully Guarded Comfort Zone

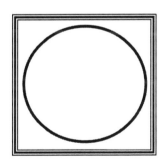

The thick circle on the left illustrates a small, carefully guarded comfort zone. If yours is like this, you will try to avoid anything that makes you feel ill at ease. This way of thinking and acting inhibits your character development.

When uncomfortable situations in relationships confront you, do you push them away because they are unsafe or unfamiliar? Avoiding new possibilities limits your personal and spiritual growth.

Permeable Comfort Zone

The illustration on the right illustrates someone who has a permeable comfort zone. He allows uncomfortable events into his life. As a result, his circle is constantly morphing as he grows to incorporate new experiences.

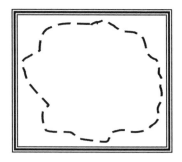

NOTE: You may have a combination of both types of comfort zones. For example, you may have areas of your life where you are not open to change, but are willing to change in others.

Draw what you think your comfort zone looks like right now.

What would you like your comfort zone to be like?

Second Corinthians 5:17 (ESV) says, "If anyone is in Christ, he is a new creation. The old has passed away; behold, the new has come."

The *New Living Translation* says, "Anyone who belongs to Christ has become a new person. The old life is gone; a new life has begun!"

What might you need to change to be able to explore and apply God's Word on a deeper level?

Scripture Translations Used

Other Books by the Author

Most of the books are written by Gaylyn. Some are co-authored with Ken Williams, PhD, Gaylyn's father. They are noted.

Some of these books are also available as online courses at http://rrcourses.com.

- *Never Do Fundraising Again*
- *Stress Busters for Missionaries, also called, All Stressed Up and Everywhere to Go!*
- *Boost Your Relationship IQ, also called, God's Design for Community*
- *Never Fear Conflict Again, also called, Reconcilable Differences*

Boost Your Relationship IQ

By Gaylyn R. Williams and Ken Williams, Ph.D.

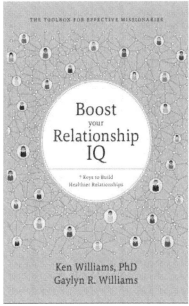

We live in a variety of communities, including family, church, mission, ministry, team and more. How we relate to one another will demonstrate whether we are living in ways that glorify God. One of our goals should be to interact with the people in our lives so they will be drawn to God, us and our communities.

In this practical, biblical book you will discover how to:

- Cultivate strong communities that glorify God and draw people to Him and to your group--both believers and not-yet believers
- Deepen your personal knowledge of the Bible
- Grow in your relationship with God
- Learn how to live out God's Word in all your relationships
- Discover step-by-step, practical applications to enrich your life
- Develop effective communication expertise to deepen your connections
- Discern what others are communicating to you, both verbally and nonverbally
- Challenge your personal and community core beliefs
- Build rapport with others quickly, to enhance your interactions and communication
- Create receptivity to your ideas
- Establish a bond of trust resulting in long-term, meaningful associations
- Break free of your fears and the security of your comfort zone, pushing you beyond whatever hinders your relationships

This is the first book in this series. Learn how you can get it free at www.GodsDesignForCommunity.com

This is based on the book and subsequent workshops called *Sharpening Your Interpersonal Skills* written by Ken and Gaylyn Williams, a father-daughter team. Gaylyn, as well as Ken and his wife Bobbie, served with Wycliffe Bible Translators.

This book is divided into seven Keys to unlock relationships:

1. *Lay the Foundation* unlocks the connection between how God sees us and how we treat others.

2. *STOP in the Name of Love!* unlocks readers' potential by helping them stop sabotaging their relationships.

3. *Listen Up* unlocks understanding.

4. *Unravel the Mystery* unlocks intimacy in relationships.

5. *Nurture Trust unlocks a healthy foundation for relationships*

6. *Cultivate Life* unlocks the power of encouragement.

7. *Overcome Obstacles* solidifies the skills learned.

Each Key examines a skill you can apply to relationships with anyone in your communities—family members, friends, colleagues and even acquaintances. As you complete the activities, your communication skills and knowledge of Scripture will be strengthened.

Available as a book, online course or workshop for your ministry.
www.RelationshipResources.org; www.RRcourses.com

Breakthrough Strategies for Every Believer

A Biblical Guide to Spiritual Warfare

Do you feel confused, overwhelmed, fearful or defeated?

Uncover simple ways to overcome Satan's strategies and embrace God's victory.

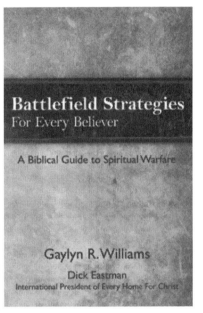

God has already won the war against the enemy and given us our handbook with the winning strategies— the Bible. The enemy comes to steal, kill and destroy, but Jesus came to give us a rich and satisfying life (John 10:10).

This easy-to-apply exploration of spiritual warfare will prepare you to

- Overcome anything hindering you from success in your life.
- Expose the devil's playbook and render his tactics powerless.
- Protect yourself and your family with powerful, strategic prayers.
- Exchange bondage for the freedom Christ purchased on the cross.
- Demystify the enemy and spiritual warfare biblically and effectively.

This biblical guidebook empowers you to successfully block Satan's assaults today and every day. It is filled with Scripture, Bible study questions and proven principles, inspiring individuals and small groups to live victorious lives.

You'll discover greater power and authority as you focus on God rather than Satan.

Quotes from the Foreword
by Dick Eastman, International President, Every Home for Christ

"In encountering *Battlefield Strategies*, I was struck by the fact that these very practices—the prayer strategies I've been using in my personal prayer life as well as in the EHC ministry—are just what Gaylyn Williams describes as "battlefield strategies" for victorious spiritual warfare.

From years of my own experience, and in reading the experiences of mighty prayer warriors of past generations, I can tell you that the principles and strategies Gaylyn Williams shares truly work. They work on a global scale, releasing victory in the nations, and they can work in your life personally as you seek the Lord's victory in your own circumstances. When we are equipped to engage in spiritual warfare effectively, we truly become agents of transformation. And it begins with transformation in our own lives.

Battlefield Strategies is a resource, a guide you'll want to return to again and again as you encounter new circumstances and battles and need new strategies to face them. *Battlefield Strategies* is practical and engaging, with biblical insights woven together by an author who has faced her own share of difficult battles and emerged victorious in Christ. Gaylyn's humor and willingness to share from her heart and life will surely encourage you as you learn to walk in victory.

Most of all, I am impressed by *Battlefield Strategies* because of its holistic approach and its clear focus on Jesus. Gaylyn thoroughly explores what the Bible has to say, not just about spiritual warfare, but about every aspect that relates to our participation in it. Although much has been written on the topic of spiritual warfare, I believe Gaylyn's work is unique and uniquely powerful because of her insistent focus on Christ, His power and His already accomplished victory rather than on the enemy. This is significant.

I encourage you to immerse yourself in *Battlefield Strategies* and embrace these proven principles for your life. Study the Scriptures, ponder the questions, meditate on the lessons, and pray the practical prayers in each chapter. Read it on your own and read it with a small group or your family. Then, watch how God responds as you apply these biblically proven *Battlefield Strategies* in your own life."

Stress Busters for Missionaries

Tools to Balance Your Life and Reclaim Your Peace

By Gaylyn R. Williams and Ken Williams, Ph.D.

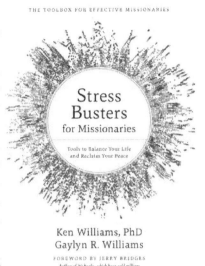

THE TOOLBOX FOR EFFECTIVE MISSIONARIES

Stress Busters for Missionaries

Tools to Balance Your Life and Reclaim Your Peace

Ken Williams, PhD
Gaylyn R. Williams

FOREWORD BY JERRY BRIDGES
Author of 23 books, which have sold millions

From the daily hassles to the catastrophic events, this book will empower you to successfully de-stress your life and recover your sanity. You'll discover easy-to-use skills enabling you to gain greater freedom from life's ups and down.

In today's fast-paced, overworked world, stress is all around us: the economy, finances, raising children, health, job, school, family or lack of it, elderly parents, divorce, tragedy, debt, death and conflict.

This is not an ordinary book about stress!

This unique workbook contains practical, biblical tools for attaining spiritual, emotional, physical and interpersonal balance. It is filled with powerful personal stories to illustrate principles, thought-provoking questions for individual or group study, Bible studies, self-assessments and easy-to-apply strategies to develop a balanced lifestyle.

As you explore the timeless connection between biblical principles and this practical, life-enhancing approach, you'll gain valuable solutions to cope with your own stress, as well as help friends and family.

These powerful strategies have been proven worldwide. Over twenty thousand pastors and ministry leaders in eighty countries have benefitted from these life-changing skills. Ken and Gaylyn first tested them in their own lives and continue to use them on a regular basis.

Rather than writing from a clinical perspective—although Dr. Williams, with his PhD in Human Behavior, could do that—they honestly share their personal experiences, having each dealt with numerous major and minor stresses. They have trained people in Christian organizations in these methods for twenty-five years. Now they are available to you.

What others are saying about this book:

"I recommend you take the time to read this important book. The Biblical solutions and personal truths in this book can set your heart, mind and soul free. This book is a timely remedy for a culture consumed with pressure, over-scheduling, impossible deadlines and sleepless nights full of anxiety."
—*Gary Wilkerson, President of World Challenge*

"Dr. Ken Williams and his daughter, Gaylyn, have teamed up to provide an excellent resource for believers who want to de-stress their lives through the application of God's Word mixed with healthy counseling principles."
—*Bob Creson, President and CEO, Wycliffe Bible Translators USA*

"*All Stressed up and Everywhere to Go* is a refreshingly simple book filled with usable, practical advice in dealing with the stressors of life."
—*George Stahnke, Director of Renewal Ministries*

"The principles work! Because the principles flow out of God's Word, they are timeless and relevant in any context. The principles are easy to grasp and easy to hand off to others who are in the 'stress crucible.'"
—*Tim Westcott, Pastor of Idyllwild Bible Church*

"This father/daughter writing team have produced something profoundly useful for the Christian community. Authentic, soundly practical, occasionally funny, often heart-wrenching—you'll love it!"
—*Laura Mae Gardner, D.Min., International Training Consultant for Wycliffe Bible Translators and SIL International*

"[This book] equips one to develop strategies and skills for managing stress in a life giving manner."
—*Wayne Cone, Pastor of Pastoral Care, Cypress Bible Church*

"This book is the best material I have found on handling stress. The principles are solidly Biblical. They are born out of real life experience facing stress."
—*Steven G. Edlin MA LCPC MFT, Counseling Director, TEAM*

"I commend the book to all who are involved in Christian service, however, every believer would benefit from this material."
—*Frank Hoskin, Director, Wycliffe Bible Translators Australia*

Keys to Joy

How to Unlock God's Gifts of Lasting Happiness

By Gaylyn R. Williams and Ken Williams, Ph.D.

Discover Thirteen Surprising, Proven Secrets To Unlock Your Joy!

Experiencing joy is a natural—but often elusive—part of Christian living. The hurts of life, unhelpful habits and unhealthy attitudes all lock out joy for many believers. And it remains locked until they take action to open it up.

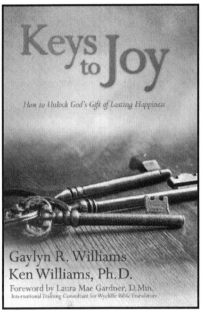

Keys to Joy not only shows you the door, but gives you the keys you need to usher yourself daily into the full, lasting joy God offers. You'll discover how to:

- Climb to new heights of joy in your relationships with God, family and others;
- Replace worry and fear with peace and contentment;
- Demolish unhappiness, misery and discouragement;
- Eradicate anything that locks joy out of your life;
- Transform trials into stepping stones.

In this practical, life-changing Bible study, you'll uncover strength and encouragement for your difficult times through the authors' powerful stories of God's joy in sufferings. Each daily study includes Scriptures with questions to contemplate and grow in your relationship with God. They are designed to empower you to experience the full joy God has for you.

Keys to Joy is for individuals, couples or small groups, and includes a leader's guide for group study. It provides the biblical understanding and life patterns you need to live joyfully regardless of your struggles. Once you've opened the door to joy, you'll know how to assure it's never shut again.

What people are saying about *Keys to Joy*:

"John records a wonderful statement made by Jesus, 'I have told you these things so that you will be filled with my joy. Yes, your joy will overflow' John 15:11 NLT). Jesus wants our joy to overflow. What are these things that Jesus spoke of? In this book, *Keys to Joy*, Ken and Gaylyn Williams, the father-daughter writing team, do us a favor by reminding us of the things that lead to joy in the Christian life. Based on the study of God's Word, the contents of this book will lead the reader to a greater sense of who God is, and a deep abiding peace in the One who loves us and wants a relationship with his children."

—*Bob Creson, President/CEO of Wycliffe Bible Translators USA*

"In the midst of a world filled with broken promises and elusive dreams, *Keys to Joy* provides powerful clarity to obtaining lasting joy. Each chapter contains poignant narrative packed with spiritual truth and practical application. Everyone desires joy, but few discover the key to obtaining it. *Keys to Joy* unlocks the mystery of joy's obscurity by providing 12 surprising truths. It's a must read for every avid 'joy' seeker."

—*Julie Gorman, Founder and Executive Director for FYI*

"Joy is one of the fruits of the spirit which I find so challenging to allow to grow in my life, especially during times of uncertainty and pain. Guilt and condemnation seem to follow during these difficult times. With much hope, Gaylyn and Ken, share not only their personal struggles on their journey to joy, but practical steps to allow joy to flourish in even the most challenging times."

—*Evelyn Sherwood, Wife, mother, grandmother and pastor's wife*

"This book is eminently practical, thoroughly Biblical, thirst-promoting. It fills me with eagerness to study it more and enthusiastic about promoting it. It is a super book!!!! I can't say enough good things about it."

—*Laura Mae Gardner, D.Min., International Training Consultant for Wycliffe Bible Translators*

"'The choice to rejoice.' That phrase reverberates in my heart since reading this delightful, scriptural study on the keys to joy. Ken and Gaylyn share personal experiences and give practical, biblical advice (keys) to help believers unlock the door to true joy."

—*Steven Sherwood Sr., Pastor of Fairview Baptist Church*

The Surprising Joy of Exploring God's Heart

A Daily Adventure with 365 of His Names

Embark on a Life-Changing Adventure!

Do you long to fall deeper in love with God? Would you like to come into His presence in new and fresh ways? In as little as five minutes a day, enhance your intimacy with God as you explore His names.

This powerful, daily devotional and journal will help you:

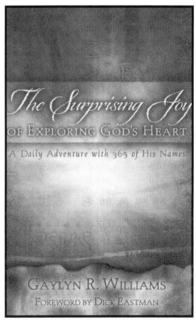

- Discover new insights into your awesome God;
- Experience comfort, strength and hope from understanding God's character;
- Expand your vision for God's power, majesty and greatness;
- Enjoy a growing passion for God through praise and worship;
- Transform your prayer life and strengthen your faith.

This unique treasure contains 365 names of God directly from the Bible. Uncover daily encouragement as you dig deeper into who God is and how He relates to you personally.

Individuals, couples, families and small groups can use this simple yet powerful tool to climb to new heights in your relationship with God and others. You'll be forever changed as you get to know God in new ways.

This book is also available as a journal, with only the Name of God, a verse and the reference. The rest of the page is blank for you to write your thoughts.

What others are saying about this book:

"In this series, Gaylyn Williams has done a remarkable job of identifying and explaining the various names God uses to describe Himself. Meditating on these names, one day at a time, will help us to know God more intimately."

Jerry Bridges, Author of twelve books, including, Trusting God

"Knowing the names of God is to know the heart of God. Gaylyn helps us know God better by revealing his character and nature. Take the time to read this book and you will be changed."

Gary Wilkerson, President, World Challenge

"This exceptional daily devotional reveals God's character. When we draw closer to Him, 'blessings' happen."

Chuck Asay, Syndicated Editorial Cartoonist

"I urge you, to use this book along with your Bible, read it daily, study it and meditate on Him, the God who is Love (1John 4:16). As I studied this book, I oft found myself laughing, shouting and crying with joy as the Holy Spirit would overwhelm me with the greatness of Who God is."

Steven R Sherwood, Sr. Pastor Fairview Baptist Church, Kokomo, IN

"These brief meditations are geared specifically to the contemporary believer's busy life. Gaylyn shares 365 ways God is addressed in Scripture. And she invites busy Christians (me...you) to engage in understanding God more intimately. These brief, to the point page-long meditations and Gaylyn's questions urge the reader toward application to personal life in the 21st Century."

Sandra T. Auer, Campus Crusade for Christ, Member Care

"We will never grow beyond our revelation of who God is. Everything in our lives flows from our understanding of the character and attributes of God. One of the best ways to grow in our relationship with God is to grow in our understanding of His names. This book is a great tool to become more intimately acquainted with the many facets of God's character by praying into and thinking deeply upon the names of God."

Jayde Duncan, Senior Pastor of Freedom Church in Colorado Springs

Never Do Fundraising Again

You Really Can Transform Donors into Lifelong Partners

By Ken Williams, Ph.D. and Gaylyn Williams

In this practical, biblical book you will discover how to:

- Convert one time gifts into lifetime support
- Experience the amazing power of gratitude to motivate people
- Employ effective communication skills—both written and verbal
- Transform the stress and drudgery of fundraising into a joyful ministry
- Utilize proven strategies to spend less time, effort and money to maintain full support
- Cultivate life-long ministry partners and close friends
- Inspire your partners to become your best recruiters for more support
- Enjoy freedom from worry about your financial needs

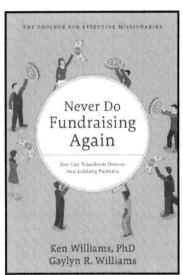

Never Do Fundraising Again contains over 200 pages of proven strategies and skills for building and maintaining your support. It is filled with powerful stories from the author's lives and others who are using the biblical principles.

This book is written by Ken and Gaylyn Williams, a father-daughter team with over 85 years' experience (combined) as supported missionaries. Gaylyn, as well as Ken and his wife Bobbie, served with Wycliffe Bible Translators.

Look what others are saying about this book:

"An outstanding book, applying Biblical principles to partner development."
Ken Royer, D.Min., Director of Pastoral Care, Link Care Center Fresno, CA

"I was amazed by this book. It is so practical and is the right way to do these things."
Laura Mae Gardner, D.Min., International Training Consultant for Wycliffe Bible Translators

"This book reflects our core belief about the types of relations needed for sustainable, effective work (and life in general). Thanks for helping us understand resource realities (finances) in light of relational resiliency (friendships). Your use of metaphors, examples, Scripture and suggestions really help to make the material practical."

Dr. Kelly O'Donnell and Dr. Michèle Lewis O'Donnell, Consulting Psychologists, Member Care Associates, Inc.

"We are excited to see these principles now in print! And this book contains many ideas and examples of ministering to your partnership team."

Dr. Jim and Jan Holsclaw, Wycliffe Bible Translators

"This book is a wonderful description of biblical partnership for ministry! Gaylyn and Ken share a very practical and God-honoring lifestyle of relating to ministry partners that goes far beyond fundraising. I heartily recommend this resource to all involved in ministry today."

Paul Lere, International Training Partners

"This book is a must read, if you are a missionary, no matter if you have just begun fundraising or have been doing it for a long time! It has been a joy to learn from these giants who attend so beautifully to their ministry partners. May those who read this workbook carefully consider its godly principles of partner-caring."

Dick and Vicki Gascho, Greater Europe Mission

"This book is tangible evidence of Ken and Gaylyn's commitment to Scripture. This book is thoroughly biblical, and chock-full of Scripture. Their ideas and suggestions are so biblically based. The book is also thoroughly practical. There are enough ideas to keep one busy for a lifetime. It is with much joy (one of Ken's and Gaylyn's favorite words) that I recommend this book to everyone who is called by God to discover and serve together with partners."

Dr. and Mrs. Jim Van Meter, with Paraclete Mission Group

2031 Names of God

Transform Your Life as You Get to Know God in New Ways

Enhance Your Intimacy with God as You Explore His Names

Do you long for to know God better? This simple, yet powerful book will help you:

- Experience the fullness of your awesome God through His names revealed in his Word
- Come into God's presence in new and fresh ways
- Discover comfort, strength and hope from understanding God's character
- Expand your vision for God's power, majesty and greatness
- Enjoy a growing passion for God through praise and worship Transform your prayer life and strengthen your faith

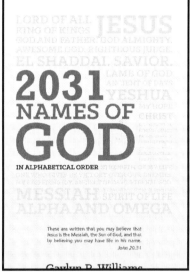

This unique treasure has 2031 names of God directly from the Bible, along with Scripture references and over 400 Greek or Hebrew names. Uncover daily encouragement as you dig deeper into who God is and how He relates to you personally. You'll be forever changed as you get to know God in new ways.

This life-changing reference book will empower:

- individuals, couples and families wanting to grow in their relationship with God small groups desiring a unique study
- pastors preparing for sermons
- college and seminary students doing research for classes
- missionaries seeking to maintain their love for God in difficult situations

This book is available in alphabetical order and in Scriptural order.

What others are saying about *2031 Names of God:*

"Gaylyn has compiled the powerful Names of God into a study guide for our spiritual growth. Philippians 3:7-8 declares Paul's heart to know Him "But whatever gain I had, I counted as loss for the sake of Christ. Indeed, I count everything as loss because of the surpassing worth of knowing Christ Jesus my Lord..." Proverbs 18:10 declares "The name of the LORD is a strong tower; the righteous man (or woman) runs into it and is safe." How much we need to know His Names to know His heart for us as His children! Be blessed as you study this compilation of His Character as revealed by His Names."

Camilla L. Seabolt, Former Executive Director of Community Bible Study

"We serve an amazing God! Understanding and appreciating the character of the Lord is the beginning of knowing who we are in Him. In Gaylyn Williams' *2031 Names of God,* she explores and uncovers who God is by examining the 2031 names given to the Lord. As a military retiree who spent 30 years serving my Nation and my Lord, how refreshing it will be to those who serve to discover in a more intimate way the Lord they serve through this journey Gaylyn will take you on."

Brig General David B. Warner, USAF (Ret.), Executive Director, Officers'
Christian Fellowship

"This wonderful collection of Names of our Lord that has been compiled by a special friend of my wife and me, Gaylyn Williams. You will find literally hundreds and hundreds of such descriptive expressions in Scripture in the pages that follow. Indeed, the author of this helpful guide has saved you countless hours in searching out these cherished expressions describing the nature and character of our Lord."

Dick Eastman, International President of Every Home for Christ

"This book is beyond amazing! What a treasure! I've considered myself a serious student of Scripture for 60 years, but had no idea of the richness of God's revelation about who He is. This book will be a companion to my Bible reading and devotional times from now on, as I come to appreciate even more God's rich character."

Ken Williams, Ph.D., fifty-five year Missionary with Wycliffe Bible Translators

The Surprising Joy of Discovering How God Sees You

A Daily Adventure with Your Identity in Christ

Many people devote their lives to seeking love and approval from their relationships, possessions, career or appearance. True love and acceptance can only be found in God when you understand and believe what He says about you.

This unique treasure, revealing 365 truths about how God sees you, will

- Enable you to grasp God's image shaped in you
- Change how you live your life as you experience more of God's love
- Empower you to reach your full potential and recognize your great worth in God's eyes
- Increase confidence, understanding and acceptance in your life and relationships
- Stimulate an awareness of the power and authority in your life
- Encourage discovery of your destiny—what God created you to do

Uncover daily encouragement as you dig deeper into Scripture, discovering what God says about you. These devotional studies contain powerful Bible verses, personal illustrations, relevant prayers, thought-provoking questions and challenging meditations.

You'll be forever changed as you discover your true identity in Christ.

This life-changing book will inspire pastors preparing sermons; small groups desiring a unique study; college and seminary students doing research; ministry leaders communicating God's love to those they serve; and individuals, couples and families wanting to better understand themselves and others.

Also available as a journal.

What Others Are Saying about *The Surprising Joy of Discovering How God Sees You:*

"I truly believe in the utmost importance of spending daily time with the Lord in prayer and in His Word. *The Surprising Joy of Discovering How God Sees You* is an incredible resource for seeking and connecting with the heart of God during those daily times. Filled with Scripture, insightful thoughts, and probing questions, this book will deepen your understanding and awareness of God's love for you, help you discover who you are in Him, and guide you in 'walking out' that identity from day to day. Every page of Gaylyn's work is, as always, marked with her wisdom, encouraging spirit, and genuine love for the reader. This is a book I will be coming back to for years to come."

Dick Eastman, International President of Every Home for Christ

"I highly recommend Gaylyn's treasures taken straight from the Scriptures! I am reminded of the passage in Ephesians: 'Christ also loved the church and gave Himself up for her, so that He might sanctify her, having cleansed her by the washing of water with the word,' (Ephesians 5:25–26 NASB). Gaylyn's compilation of the Word of God with applications on 'How God Sees You' is vital for each of us. As you and I spend daily time in this resource, we will be reminded afresh of who we are in Christ. The result will be evidenced in our lives by greater cleansing, intimacy and power with our Lord. You will relish the time you spend sitting with Him and pondering these passages and principles. Get ready for wonderful times of refreshing from the Holy Spirit!"

Camilla Leathers Seabolt, Former Executive Director for Community Bible Study

"Until we understand our true identity as a child of God, we will never feel whole. Working on this book gave me a new appreciation for who I am in Christ. It taught me that God is the missing piece to everything that we lack. To the fatherless, He is a father. To the weak, He is strength. In this way, the book can be useful to anyone who feels inadequate in some form or another. As a teenager in this world of media and persuasion, I often feel less than. By learning my birthright in God's kingdom, I realized that

I have access to everything that He is. My power lies in Him; therefore, I am capable of anything."

Kacie Linamen, Teenager and College Student

"Gaylyn Williams presents in this book an eternal treasure chest of who God is and how He desires to spiritually refresh us. It's a great book to encourage you on your walk with the Lord."

—*Steve Koeppen, President, Living Way Ministries, Colorado Springs*

"As ever, Gaylyn's newest guide to applying specific Scripture portions to life is both practical and specific. Use these daily devotionals as a guide for your quiet time with Jesus or as a script for a small group studying the Bible together. Keeping a journal of your responses could be useful for later reference. However you choose to use it, this book of devotionals is bound to bless you, those you live with and those you minister to."

—*Sandra T. Auer, Cru Human Resources Specialist and Counselor*

"Just being able to do the research and looking up verses allowed me to finally realize who I am in Christ. The biggest benefit was knowing who I am in Christ based on what the Word said. Another benefit was doing the research knowing that all of this was going to be put into a book. It allowed me to dig into the Word more."

—*Rubin Paxton, Ministry Partner*

The Surprising Joy of Embracing God's Promises

365 Reminders of His Faithfulness

Have you lived with broken promises, wondering whom you can trust?

The Bible is filled with hundreds of promises you can claim for your life.

Discover 365 reminders of God's faithfulness—something for any situation you may face. In as little as five minutes a day, you can enhance your intimacy with God as you explore His promises.

This powerful, daily devotional will help you:

- recognize God's amazing faithfulness as He keeps His promises
- find new hope, comfort, joy and peace
- transform your prayer life and strengthen your faith
- discover new insights about your awesome God
- learn to appreciate God's presence and protection

This simple study can have a lifetime impact. You'll find Scriptures to meditate on, practical applications, powerful stories, prayers to guide you and truths to declare.

You'll be forever changed as you learn to fully embrace God's promises.

This life-changing book will inspire pastors, small groups, ministry leaders, individuals, couples and families wanting to better understand God's faithfulness.

Also available as a journal.

Snapshots

At the end of each topic, prayerfully consider one or two things you believe God wants you to take away. Note them in the appropriate snapshot section.

You can do any of the following:

- Write down one or two things you want to remember or work on from this chapter.
- Summarize the key points that stood out to you.
- Jot down your insights and reactions.

This section is extremely important for your learning process. It provides you with one place to review what you learned. It may become a "to do" list for what you want to work on from each chapter. Don't skip this section. It is critical for transforming your relationships.

Chapter 1: All You Need Is Love

Chapter 2: Conflict Is Inevitable, but Combat Is Optional

Chapter 3: Fight a Winning Battle

Chapter 4: How Am I at Managing Conflicts?

Chapter 5 How Can Conflict Improve My Relationships?

Chapter 6: A Call to Engage

Chapter 7: Rules of Engagement

Chapter 8: How Am I at Confronting?

Chapter 9: How Can I Confront More Effectively?

Chapter 10: Defuse a Ticking Time Bomb

Chapter 11: How Do I Respond to Verbal Attacks?

Chapter 12: How Can I Respond Better When I'm Attacked?

Chapter 13: One on One

Printed in Great Britain
by Amazon

56981149R00170